Believe - Do You?

What people are saying . . . .

Phyllis takes you on her personal journey discovering her abilities, from her family history to her journey in embracing her incredible mediumship abilities — and her courage to sharing it with the world. She is genuine, vulnerable, and informative. Not only will you learn how our loved ones connect with us from the beyond through Phyllis, but you'll also learn the profound love and wisdom they impart, as well. Her book is an easy, entertaining, and fascinating read. And, of course, Phyllis is amazing!

— Donna Russo, owner of Heart Soul Intuitive

A compelling read to show us how the most important part about embracing your intuitive gifts is trusting yourself. Phyllis takes us on a journey of discovery to show us how her spiritual gifts developed, illustrating that even though the Universe can guide, YOU have to take the first step. It's time to believe. . . .

— Jeff Carpenter, Spirit Rescue Medium and author
Discovering Intention: A Sensitive's Guide to the Engineering Mind

Believe — Do You? *encapsulates Phyllis's humor and energy as all her friends and family know her to be. Each chapter captures a bird's eye view of life as a psychic as well as lends the reader an opportunity to act as a voyeur, peering into the intimate behind the scenes moments and memoirs of someone with the ability to harness extra sensory abilities. Despite Phyllis's superpowers, she is one of the most grounded, genuine, and relatable women I know and have the honor of calling my friend. I hope this book debunks the stigma surrounding the supernatural and that readers get lost in the humble meanderings of an everyday person who chose to courageously and openly share her gifts so she can help others. I have the privilege of sharing a dual relationship with Phyllis, both personally and professionally, and can attest to her honest, burning desire to serve with purpose and passion. Don't take my word for it. Read the book!*

— Kerry Holzschuh, Client, Friend and Supporter

Believe — Do You? *is an engaging book about self-revelation, courage, confidence, and a belief in oneself. Phyllis accepts the encouragement from family, friends, peers, and her mentors from another realm to help with her struggle to decide to become a medium. She tells us her story of how she becomes strong enough to allow herself to feel comfortable with sharing her intuitiveness with others and how her family background began her journey. This is a great read to encourage anyone to change and do what makes them feel happy. I enjoyed reading this book and feel Phyllis's great desire to help others. She is an inspiration, and this book will make you excited to try and do new things to get where Phyllis is today.*

— Brenda Eng-Bott, Friend

Read this book and make an analogy between the author's psychic development and your own situations that may indicate your potential abilities. Enlightening information about our everyday experiences, involving our intuitive abilities and messages provided to us from those who have passed on.

— Michelle, Mentor

Believe — Do You? *is an approachable and readable book and not easy to put down once started. The reader indeed learns ways to open oneself to the possibility of the unknown through the experiences the author Phyllis Mitchell has encountered and presented. But more importantly, the characters Mitchell describes become our friends and family members and are relatable to the people we know. One can reflect on what the author presents and ponder what important lessons presented can enrich the reader's life. It's not only our intuitiveness that can be opened but other self-worthy lessons to enrich our life.*

— Lynn, Mentor

Phyllis Mitchell opens the book with the line "To believe is a choice." And for the rest of the book she brings you down her journey to fully understanding that statement.

Belief in yourself, your truth, the afterlife, in others. It is a beautiful message that she weaves throughout her exploration into her own belief not only in her powers but in the belief that those powers are her gifts to the world not just to herself.

Even if you are not a believer in the afterworld, this book gives hope and proof that believing, if in nothing else other than yourself, will grant you the permission to find your true passion and allow your own truth to shine through.

I have had a reading twice by Phyllis and she has a true gift of intuition and beyond.

Thank you for writing your truth.

— Nicole, Client

When picking up a book about a psychic medium, one may expect to be carried away to a dark world of outrageous scenarios, freaky stories, and over-the-top characters. But I did not find a societal outcast in this book; I was surprised and delighted to find a kind, generous, second-generation Italian American, middle class, suburbanite woman . . . who also just so happens to be a third generation "veil," a.k.a. . . . a fortune teller!

From her, understandably, hesitant but generous assistance with murder investigations to her hilarious, light-hearted descriptions of ornery relatives unexpectedly making their presence known from the other side, this book makes one thing perfectly clear; Phyllis always uses her gift to help others.

This book was a joy to read! I was thoroughly entertained and I "just know" you will also enjoy her story!

— Renee, Songwriter

Believe - Do You?

A Psychic Medium's Journey

Phyllis Mitchell

Names marked with an * have been changed to protect the privacy of individuals.

Cover Design: Venus Raneri
Photo of Phyllis Mitchell: Venus Raneri
Cover Model: Gabrielle Elia

ISBN 978-1-7356178-0-0 (print)
ISBN 978-1-7356178-1-7 (e-book)
ISBN 978-1-7356178-2-4 (audio)

Third Eye Publishers
34 Carriage Way
Millstone Township, NJ 08510

Printed and bound in the United States of America

This book is dedicated to my family, your family, and all families.
Family is the starting point to our journey of believing.

ACKNOWLEDGEMENTS

I will start with my husband to thank. You BELIEVED in my intuitive abilities right from the start. You are the one who suggested I write a book about my journey. We have experienced life's roller coaster rides together throughout our thirty years of marriage. I am truly grateful for all you have done to love and support me in a myriad of ways. I pray you realize the depth of my love.

I want to thank my two children. Both of you are God-given blessings in my life. I appreciate your support even when we do not agree. I am proud of each of you for speaking your truths and understanding mine. I love you both with all my heart and soul.

Claudine Wolk and Julie Murkette, you call yourselves book shepherds. I must agree, for without you both, I would have been lost or led astray. The two of you helped me with editing, marketing, mentoring, and inspiring, to name a few. I admire both of your sensational skills! The two of you helped make my dream come true. A sincere THANK YOU for your honesty, direction, and dedication.

Venus Raneri, you are a visionary combining your intelligence and creativity. I will be forever grateful for your extraordinary artistic abilities and generosity. You made my vision real and enhanced it to make it surreal. I am in awe of your magical talents. I truly appreciate you being my guiding star!

Andrea Harrison, thank you for starting me off with my editing journey. You brought clarity to my story and did so with finesse. I am appreciative of your skills, and you were a pleasure to work with.

I am thankful to everyone who has touched my life and helped me learn lessons. Each of you are part of my story, even though I may not have written about you.

Those alive and departed, taught me. Gratitude and love helped me to believe.

Table of Contents

Prologue

To believe is a choice. I can't make that decision for you. Only you can do that for yourself. All I can tell you is from my experience. I can share how I came to believe and then became an even bigger believer. One focus is to believe in the dead - the oh so controversial topic of life after death; more specifically, intuition and communicating with the dead. The other focus is to believe in the living, or actually, believing in yourself.

Have you ever jumped out of your comfort zone instead of simply thinking about doing it? Have you ever made one of your dreams come true, despite thinking it didn't seem possible? That's what happened to me!

My journey of self-realization, intuition, and life after death was something I wanted to share with others. It follows the mantra I've lived by throughout my entire life: HELPING PEOPLE IS MY PASSION! I felt compelled to write my story to get people thinking, questioning, and realizing their own take on these topics.

I have always thought about writing a book. I do enjoy writing, although it's a struggle, like a love-hate relationship. When the words flow, I love it! When they don't, I hate it and wonder, "*Why even bother? This is killing me!*"

Deep down inside, I know this story needs to be told. Do you know how sometimes you just *know* something? That's your intuition talking! Mine sure screamed at me.

I cannot take all the credit for writing this book because I did not write it alone. I have my spirit guide, Marissa, who has helped me, along with my loved ones who passed before me. I do feel humbled that God has guided me. This book is for believers, nonbelievers, and those in between, regarding inner and outer spirits. My hope is that each person comes to his or her own conclusion about believing.

Chapter 1
Carmella

This story must start with my maternal grandmother Carmella. She died when I was only four years old. Stories about her have been passed down to me by family members.

Carmella was an Italian woman who came to the United States at the innocent age of fourteen in January 1907. She turned fifteen that February. As the story from my relatives goes, Carmella was sent to marry one of two men. The first man was older and owned a grocery store. The other was a younger man, with not as much money. Her choice defined her. She chose Frank, the man with the money. Money was an essential part of her life.

When Carmella was sixteen, she married Frank, who was twenty-four. Within a year, she gave birth to my Uncle Louie. My grandmother worked in her husband's grocery store, although that didn't satisfy her. Carmella was a true pioneer, a woman ahead of her time. She was born with a *veil.* In Italian culture, it means to be gifted as a *seer*, one who can tell the future. She was a *fortuneteller*, since she was born in the late 1800s, the word *psychic* wasn't common. Using her *gift*, she started out reading tea leaves and tarot cards for people in her home, which was above the grocery store. The number of clients kept multiplying, so she opened her **own** business, "Lena's Tea Room," which was named for her second child, Rachael, nicknamed Lena.

Her store was in Paterson, New Jersey, back in its heyday, close to the courthouse in town. Carmella's business blossomed by word of mouth. Her clientele was not what you would imagine, especially for the time period. My mother, the fourth child, and Uncle Tony, the fifth of Carmella's children, touted that she had judges, attorneys, and local politicians as clients. These were educated, well-respected citizens going to a fortuneteller. I kid you not! My mother and uncle saw them with their own eyes — not even with their glasses. They needed those later in life.

My cousin also told me that Carmella had priests as clients. Hearing that shocked me to the core! My cousin is quite religious, so for her to tell me that, I know it must be true. Word kept spreading of Carmella's mysterious yet accurate abilities. New York showgirls were also a part of her regular clientele. Quite impressive, even now, to have those types of clients. Back then, unheard of!

Carmella had plenty of local residents as clients, too. The numbers increased, especially during wartime, when frightened women were desperate to know if their husbands, brothers, or sons would make it back alive. Carmella was well-respected and earned a lot of money because of it.

Did her readings come true? My mother would say, "Yes." During World War II, my grandmother told my mother that she would meet and then marry a man in uniform. I bet you're thinking that you could have told her that too, and you are not a fortuneteller!

My father, Bill, was not in the military. He became a bus driver during the war as part of community service, and wore a uniform. My father was not drafted because he was the oldest son. His father had died, leaving a wife, two daughters, and three sons on the family farm. His two younger brothers went off to war wearing army uniforms, but not my father. Driving a bus is how my father met my mother. She was part of the war effort, working at DuPont, making explosives. She took his bus to get to work. They would smile at one another and make small talk. The rest, as they say, is history.

When my father first came to my grandparents' house for dinner, he loved all the different kinds of Italian food they served. My mother was all Italian. Both her mother and father were from southern Naples, in the province of Avellino. My grandmother prided herself on her native cooking. Being of

English and Dutch descent, my father, until that time, had never eaten Italian food. Yet he asked for second helpings, the food was so delicious, and he really enjoyed it.

During dinner, my mother's relatives were all speaking Italian, and my father did not understand a single word. He heard yelling, screaming, and saw hands waving wildly in the air making all kinds of gestures. He turned to my mother and said, "Are they all fighting?" My mother laughed and said, "No, just having a normal conversation." If you are of Italian descent, you probably got a good laugh out of that! My mom did admit to my dad, however, that sometimes fights did occur, and relatives would storm out of the house.

My Uncle Mike couldn't wait to permanently leave his parents' house. Once he was of age, he married and moved to Chicago. He had heart issues and, unfortunately, died at the young age of thirty-six.

My Uncle Louie, the firstborn, was a robust man and was set in his ways. He and his wife, Dolly, were definitely nonbelievers and stood strongly against Carmella's readings. That didn't stop their children, Liz and Frankie. Liz loved having her cards read and never got caught by her parents. Frankie wasn't as lucky as his sister. When Frankie's parents found out he had his cards read, all hell broke loose! Carmella never read his cards again. In hindsight, it didn't really matter. She certainly hit the nail on the head with Frankie's only reading. In summation, Carmella told him he would have a wealthy and adventurous life. I recently asked Frankie where he hasn't traveled. He stopped, thought for a moment, and said, "Nowhere!" As for the wealthy part, let's just say you can't travel all over the world and not be wealthy.

My cousin Theresa, Aunt Lena's daughter, had her cards read constantly. She was obsessed with Carmella's talents and was a dedicated believer. Aunt Lena didn't mind, but didn't have an interest in it herself. Whenever Theresa had a headache, which could be excruciating, she would ask our grandmother to get rid of it. Carmella would pray over her to cure Theresa's *malocchio*, which translated into English, means "evil eye." The Italians believed *malocchio* was a curse put upon a person that could cause headaches, ailments, or misfortunes. Once Carmella finished her prayers, Theresa would yawn and miraculously feel better. This worked every time! One time, Theresa called our grandmother when she had a headache. Carmella said prayers over the phone and was still able to cure her.

Carmella also provided the service of getting rid of *malocchio* for her clients. Today, some people still believe in *malocchio* and use different methods that include olive oil or holy water to cure it. Some people, including myself, take preventative measures and wear an evil eye bracelet, ring, or other talisman to keep it away. Superstition, for some of us, is not easy to shake!

There was another Italian element that was part of Carmella's life. You may or may not believe in "the Mob," but my Uncle Tony told me that each week some guy stopped by my grandmother's business and collected an *envelope* from her. He saw her put money in it. How much? Who knows? Some called it "Payola," meaning money for protection. There were never robberies or other kinds of trouble to be found at Lena's Tea Room — so please draw your own conclusions.

According to my Uncle Tony, giving tarot card readings to predict someone's future was illegal in the early 1900s. My grandmother could have been thrown in jail for doing so. Undercover policemen and policewomen came into her business and asked to have their cards read. Being the fortuneteller that my grandmother truly was, she knew who they really were and their intentions. She used this knowledge to her advantage by lying and telling them that she did not read tarot cards, but that she would read their tea leaves. Reading tea leaves actually was legal. Go figure! She knew every time when a cop was trying to trick her — never got that wrong — not even once. So, her business was never shut down, and she never went to jail.

Carmella was a smart woman. She was illiterate in English, but that didn't slow her down. She signed her name with an "X." She couldn't speak English very well either; it was more like "broken English." Her tarot cards were written in Italian. Her Italian clients loved conversing with her in their native language, although she did communicate well enough with her English-speaking clients. They kept coming back and spread the word.

Carmella was a successful businesswoman. She knew how money worked, and she prospered. The money she earned enabled her to buy the house she lived in and two apartments that she rented out. She also loaned money to people with an increased rate of interest. Carmella gained valuable experience earning money through her business, rental properties, and loan offerings. She definitely understood about earning money and letting her money earn for her. Not bad for a fourteen-year-old girl who came from Italy with little money, no knowledge of the language, and an arranged marriage.

Sadly though, she wasn't happy in her marriage. She liked to be in control and walked out on the man who liked to control her. She didn't divorce her husband; that was taboo! She went to live in the house she bought, and he lived in the house he bought. I guess fate stepped in, and Frank left Carmella a widow. She tried marriage once again, although her second marriage didn't last very long. My grandmother didn't trust her second husband, Jimmy. She slowly got the feeling he was primarily after her money. Carmella worked hard for her money and her money worked hard for her. She didn't want any of it taken away. Can't say I blame her.

I only vaguely remember my grandmother, even though she lived with us for a couple years after she had fallen ill. I somewhat remember making cupcakes with my mother and saying, "Let's have a party!" So, we would: my mother, grandmother, and me. My father was at work, and my siblings were at school. My grandmother would lie in her hospital bed at our house, and my mother and I would bring in the cupcakes we'd made, along with small bottles of Coca-Cola. That's the only recollection of my grandmother I ever had. It makes sense now that I enjoy parties and making cupcakes!

Sadly, Carmella died at the age of seventy-five. Since I was only four years old at the time, I never had my tarot cards or tea leaves read by her. I never got to ask her any questions about her gift or my future.

After Carmella died, my mother's family fought with my mother over money. My mother was gracious enough to have my grandmother live with our family, and she took care of her. My mother's sister and brothers did not. My father was a very loving and respectful man. He had a special bond with my grandmother. Before and during my grandmother's illness, she relied on my father to help her with her rental properties and her own house. My father was always ready, willing, and able. Unbeknownst to my parents, my grandmother had her will changed and left $10,000 (a good sum of money in 1965) to my father. The rest of her assets were split evenly among her four children. My uncle Mike had predeceased her.

My mother's siblings believed my parents had forced my grandmother to give my father the extra money. They felt cheated and betrayed, but my mother did, too. My mother always went overboard to be good and generous with her siblings.

My mother was never a liar, and neither was my father. My grandmother must have been very appreciative of all that my father did throughout her life. She probably wanted to show her appreciation in a way she knew best — money. My parents could only surmise. They truly hadn't known she had changed her will. Consequently, my mother and her siblings did not speak from that point on and parted ways.

My mother went to a psychic about a year or two after this sad event happened. The woman told her about the rift in my mother's family. She predicted that one day, in the distant future, my mother would get together again with her estranged family members. My mother didn't believe that for one second. For those she loved, my mother did so with all her heart. For those who crossed her (she believed her family did with a vengeance), she could write them off and not think twice about it. In our household, my mother's siblings were the equivalent of criminals. They broke my mother's law, so the thought of contacting them, much less associating with them, never entered our minds.

Remarkably, throughout the years, this had never happened before but, one fine day twenty years later, driving past the cemetery, my mother saw my Aunt Lena and her daughter Theresa at my grandmother's grave. Instead of telling my father to get the hell out of there, she had him stop the car. My mother and father got out, walked to the grave, and said hello. Then, my mother asked them if they wanted to come over to our house for coffee. Aunt Lena said, "Yes!"

About an hour later, I walked into the house and saw two women at our kitchen table. My mother said, "Say hello to Aunt Lena and Theresa." My mouth must have widened about ten feet as I yelled, "Whaaaaaaaaaat?" I'm surprised I didn't faint.

The psychic's prediction came true, yet my mother never elaborated on why she did what she did. I'm guessing it was because my mother mellowed with age. Three morals to this tale. One: never say never. Two: some psychics are right even if it takes twenty years to prove it, and three: forgiveness can be found in the most unlikely places. I want to stress the last moral of this story. I am grateful to my mother and admire her for teaching me a lesson by actually living the essence of forgiveness. Thank you, Mom.

Chapter 2
My Family

By now you may be wondering about my immediate family. My parents had three children. My brother Billy and my sister Pat were eighteen months apart. They grew up very close to one another, having a true camaraderie and compassion for one another. Each would fiercely fight for the other when the occasion arose. It brought them close together, and they formed a true bond that could never be broken.

Way, way, way out of the blue, thirteen years after the birth of my sister, my mother got a surprise. She was forty years old at the time. She went to the doctor because she wasn't feeling well, and it just didn't seem to go away. Lo and behold, her doctor said to her, "You're pregnant." Now I will quote the exact reply my mother had for her doctor. "You're a liar!"

She was outraged and said, in a matter-of-fact tone, "That can't be possible!" My mother didn't need the birds and the bees explained to her since she had been down that road a while ago. All I can assume since my mother never went into any intimate details, was that a miracle had happened. That miracle was me!

I was my mother's pride and joy. Luckily for me, the anger she had for the doctor turned into pure bliss when I was born. I didn't look like my mother; she had pitch-black hair and olive skin. My brother looked more like our mother, and my sister looked more like our grandmother, Carmella. I was blond and light-skinned, more like my father's Dutch side of the family. Funny though, when you looked at all three children, you could tell we were siblings.

It was well known in our family that I was my mother's favorite. Let me rephrase that — favorite girl — since my brother was her favorite before me. Please do not misinterpret my intention here. I am not bragging, just stating a fact. It was well known in our family. My mother and I (her miracle baby) had a true loving bond. My father also loved me and respected the loving bond my mother and I had. Since he understood, he was never jealous of it. He had a special bond with my sister. However, all five of us were a tight-knit family.

After my mother and her sister reconciled, I got to meet my other aunts, uncles, and cousins that we hadn't spoken to. It was the start of a beautiful relationship with them. Psychic ability ran in the family. Remember my Uncle Tony? He was the fifth child. My grandmother had also told him he had the gift. He didn't pursue tarot card reading, but he loved going to the racetrack. His friends always wanted to go with him because he had a knack for picking winners. Well, not all the time, but more often than not. Need I say more?

He lived in Florida, and I stayed connected with him primarily through the telephone. We did share some emails along the way, but a good old cordless phone (cell phones were an imagination away at the time), served as the means for our communication. Our primary topic of conversation was psychic ability. His stories about my grandmother flowed, and I just soaked it all up. He was private about his own abilities with other people, but with me, he shared inner confidences. We were kindred souls, not personally believing in our own psychic capabilities, but recognizing each other's. We unleashed the possibility, morphed it into probability, and ignited the definite. Glowing from the flames, we soared with predictions, dreams, feelings, and just *knowing*. Uncle Tony and I looked forward to each phone call, sharing our camaraderie.

Remember I mentioned my cousin Theresa earlier, you know, the one with the headaches *malocchio* Carmella cured? She found she also had psychic abilities. Hers were primarily through dreams that would relay future happenings. She had realized this ability right before Carmella died. Theresa was on vacation in Italy, and she had a dream that her mother called her and told her Carmella had died and she had to fly home for the funeral. Sadly, a day later, her dream became a reality. Carmella died the next day, and Theresa cut her vacation short to fly home to pay her condolences. That was the start of Theresa's dreams, which would foreshadow her friends' and relatives' deaths, illnesses, births of children, and other events.

My mother was psychic, too. She had a knack for "knowing" things. There was one guy I dated in college whom my mother just despised. It got to the point where she didn't allow him in our house. She "just knew" he was no good and could not be trusted. I didn't believe her. Better yet, I didn't want to believe her. We dated for a couple of months after he was forbidden on the home front. He didn't like that I was very close to my family. He spoke badly of them and tried to manipulate me into becoming more distant from them. I slowly realized that he was controlling more and more of my life. Finally, the lightbulb went on, and that was the end of that relationship. My mother's intuition was right once again.

I had a good friend, Caroline, from college. My mother really liked her and felt, if Caroline was doing something, it was good for me, too. Caroline was an accounting major. My mother desperately wanted me to major in accounting, too. I wanted no part of it. I said accounting was just too boring for me. I really wanted to major in psychology. To me, that was truly fascinating. My mother would have none of it! Throughout my college years, she kept saying I should go for accounting, but I kept fighting her on it. I graduated with a double major in Business and English from Rutgers. I guess that was somewhat of a compromise.

After graduation, I landed a job as a sales analyst. The position lasted for a few months in the sales department. For some reason I still don't understand to this day, my position was transferred to the accounting department. I remained a sales analyst, but my new boss started to give me some accounting work, too. He commented on how well I worked with accounting and encouraged me to get my degree in it. I'm not sure if my mother had a secret meeting with my new boss and bribed him or if her intuition was rearing its head. I ended up getting a master's degree in accounting. I guess I ate humble pie and let my mom get the last laugh about me "getting into accounting." She was right again. Her intuition rang true. I even sealed the deal later on by getting my CPA. That was something I would have never dreamed of in a million years. My mother just smiled and nodded with that "knowing" look.

My mother and her family weren't the only ones who had psychic abilities. My father did, too. He had dreams of different sorts. Some were of his deceased brother Benny, who died tragically at the age of twenty-one in an automobile accident. Benny came to my father in dreams and told him things my father didn't know. These messages helped my father throughout his life. My father also had dreams that solved problems for him in his waking life, especially ones that were job-related. The expression "sleep on it" sure worked for my father!

Once my grandmother passed away, my sister Pat discovered that she had the ability to see dead people. One night, Pat woke up and saw my grandmother's face, with her glasses on, in the mirror. She wasn't afraid and felt that my grandmother was watching over her. She was comforted by this thought.

When Pat married her second husband Sal, (her first husband was abusive and not worthy of details), they lived in an apartment that seemed to be haunted. She saw a monk and other people she didn't recognize. One man turned out to be our grandfather. She had never met him in person but had seen pictures of him. She was able to handle seeing the dead; it didn't upset her. I, on the other hand, was petrified.

When I slept at her apartment, it was in a small bedroom. Pat and Sal slept on a pull-out couch in the living room. One night, I woke up and saw some shadowy figure above me. I bolted out of there as fast as I could and landed right in between Pat and Sal. I slept there for the rest of the night. I never slept over again!

Throughout her life, Pat had quite a few different houses, and she saw spirits in each one of them. She also saw one at my house when my husband and I were on a weekend getaway. We wanted to spend some quality time together without the kids. Pat was so wonderful with helping me out. When I asked if she could stay at my house to watch them, she immediately said yes.

We have a guest room, but it doesn't have a TV in it. Pat loved watching TV at night. She stayed in our bedroom with the TV. My sons were in their bedrooms. Pat was watching one of her shows and all was good, at least for a little while.

Pat happened to hear some kind of noise and, while lying in bed, she turned her head to look out my bedroom door. She saw a man dressed in what looked like a brown uniform, almost like a UPS guy, walking in the hallway. She couldn't believe her eyes and her first thought was, "*I have to protect my nephews!*" She jumped out of bed and ran to the hallway to look for the guy. She checked in the hallway, bathroom, and closet but didn't see him. She ran to each of my children's bedrooms, and they were both fast asleep with no one else in their rooms. She was so thankful they were both safe.

While walking back to the bedroom, it dawned on her that the guy who looked real could actually be a spirit . . . or a ghost! She was so relieved that he was not an actual intruder. Although, if you had asked her at first if the guy was real, she would have bet you a million dollars he was. Normally, Pat can tell the difference between spirits and humans. This guy sure fooled her! She was not sleeping over at my house again. Unlike before, this spirit really spooked her! I am thankful to say I have never seen the guy. I hope and pray that I never do!

Pat's psychic abilities would also come out in dreams. She had one dream of my grandmother that seemed real. It was as if she was actually with my grandmother again. You may have heard of these dreams referred to as *visits*. These dreams are different. They are quite vivid. The person tends to remember them very easily and has a long recall time.

I have also had this kind of dream many times. It's as if you are actually with the deceased person again. You touch them and feel them as if they are real. The dream brings you to a state of an "alternate reality." I just picked that phrase to describe it, but I cannot explain how it happens, and the feeling is incredible. It's like you get a second chance to actually be with your loved one again — for real. It is truly incredible and so very humbling to have been chosen to have this seemingly unbelievable yet believable experience.

Pat also had a great ability to just *know* things like my mother did. Many friends and relatives sought out her advice. She didn't read tarot cards, but had an innate way of knowing about things. She was excellent with first impressions. She was right about people, regarding their personalities, only shortly after meeting them; definitely a good trait to have. I know she could have read tarot cards, but chose not to. I never understood why.

My mother had "psychics" — (a word more currently used) come to our house. When I was in my early teens, I had my cards read — a natural thing to do for the women in my family. My father and brother were not into that "stuff," although the irony was that my father and brother both had psychic abilities. They just weren't into the tarot cards or medium readings.

My brother, Billy, has great intuition. It comes into play for him in different ways. One way his intuition shines is through watching sports, which he really enjoys. When he was younger, he liked to bet on sporting events. Like my Uncle Tony, he won more than he lost. He's also good at giving people advice. They sometimes listen to him, and when they don't, they end up regretting it. Billy also has dreams of passed loved ones and foretelling dreams like my father.

I also realized my ability to have dreams of passed loved ones. This ability surfaced earlier in my life. I had dreams of my sister-in-law's mother and father. Billy is married to my sister-in-law, Franny. Franny's parents were nice people. However, Franny's mother was a private person. She did not want other people to know her family's business. There were a few family secrets that she preferred to keep hidden. She didn't believe in "airing the family laundry," so to speak. After she and her husband passed away, I had dreams about them. However, they didn't make sense to me. I would call Franny and tell her the dream. Surprisingly to me, they made perfect sense to her. She later confided to me that when she was having a problem, she would ask her parents to help her. She would ask them to come to me in a dream and give her guidance. I had no idea prior to this.

Franny knew I could dream of the dead and asked her parents to come to me. However, the dreams were cryptic enough to me, so I wouldn't know "the secret problem," but Franny did and understood the guidance from the dream.

This went on for a while. Franny was happy with my ability to connect with them in a dream that would reveal answers to her, but not to me. She also liked the secrecy because she never explained to me what the dreams meant. I didn't pry either, but after a while, I was able to figure one out. This must not have been comfortable for her parents. They didn't want to expose answers I could understand. Interestingly enough, they found another way. This will be revealed later.

Chapter 3
Psychics and Mediums

The first time I had a tarot card reading, I was hooked. Sheer fascination and amazement set in with what the reader had to say. I looked upon tarot card readers (psychics) as special people with a "gift" of knowing the future. They were like superheroes to me with special powers. In my high school yearbook, my secret ambition was "To look into the future."

I visited psychics and mediums for many years, starting in my teens and continuing to the present. I still enjoy being read even though I can read myself! One of my early recollections of having someone read my tarot cards was in college. I was dating a handsome soccer player of Italian descent. The woman who read me said I would marry him. I was surprised, but not upset. After all, I was quite smitten with him. She told me about some other issues in my life, but my focus was on the handsome guy. At the time, I was very career-minded. He couldn't understand why I was so driven, and that was a major problem in our relationship. I thought we could work things out. We did try; we even broke up and got back together. However, we were never able to overcome this conflict.

The psychic's prediction did not come true. A few different conclusions can be drawn from this. One, the psychic was just not talented. Two, we have free will, and marriage did not end up being an option. Or three, there is another explanation somewhere in the middle. Regarding the first option, I have encountered some psychics who were just plain phonies. This tarnishes the reputation of psychics in general. Please keep in mind, though, "One bad apple don't spoil the whole bunch." Thank you, Michael Jackson!

Along the way, I have been read by various psychics. My mother and sister have had them at their houses. I've hosted them at my house, gone to the psychic's home, attended friends' houses, been to corporate events, and went to restaurants. I was magnetically attracted to them. I sought them out to help solve pressing problems and was always eager to hear what my future would bring. Sometimes I just went, on a lark, for the sheer fun of it.

I was lucky enough to have worked for a woman in accounting who was also intrigued with psychics. We traded stories of our experiences and looked forward to our discussions. She is a mentor to me. I admire her intelligence and compassion. She is my favorite boss, no contest. It's not only because we shared that common interest, but because she always treated me well. She truly believed in me. She believed in my accounting skills, and she believed in my intuitive abilities. She "just knew" I possessed them, even while I was still doubtful. Thank you, Sue!

Throughout all those years, it never dawned on me to try to teach myself how to read the cards or do mediumship. I think a part of it was because I had the notion that you had to be "born" with a gift. Like my grandmother who was "born" with a veil, she just knew from an early age she had that gift.

I didn't "know" early on, so I just figured I had to seek out other people. I think fear also played a part in holding me back. I was afraid that I had no abilities. I had to rely on someone else. Little did I know that it would take me until I was fifty-two years old to realize that I WAS born with a gift. I could read tarot cards and look into the future. At fifty-six, I realized I was able to receive messages from the dead that they needed to convey to their loved ones.

I have finally realized we are all born with intuition. I believe it is a matter of interest, focus, and practice. The amount of effort you put in affects how much you can bring out. Timing plays a crucial role, as well. I was a late bloomer in realizing and then utilizing my intuitive abilities. There are reasons, as we look back, as to why a particular time is the "right time."

Speaking of timing, I think now is a good time to end the suspense and get back to the story of Franny's parents and find another way to connect with Franny. Her parents led me to an older woman named Bea, who was a medium. A friend told me her reputation was excellent. I didn't want to tell Franny, the eternal skeptic, about Bea just yet. I told my sister, a true believer like me, that we had to go. We just loved this stuff!

The process to see Bea was a little strange, to say the least. You had to call to book an appointment. However, that didn't guarantee you would be read on your appointment day. You had to call the morning of the appointment to see if Bea had received a sign. If Bea didn't receive a sign, you had to schedule another appointment. No lie, my sister and I were rescheduled three times before we had an actual reading with Bea. Bea was true to her word about having to see a sign. Finally, one fine September morning, my sister and I drove together to see Bea.

We got to her house, and her husband let us in. He told us he would sit in the waiting room with one person while the other person was read. I'm not exactly sure why, but we just did what we were told. Bea came out and asked who the driver was. I said I was, so she told us that I was to be read first. She said I would need to build up my energy again before I drove, so I had to go first. My sister and I looked at one another, smiled, and off I went to another room.

Bea had a British accent since she was born and raised in England. She met her American husband during the war. He had been injured, and she was his nurse. She was engaged to another fellow at the time, but her husband said to himself, this is the woman I am going to marry. I wondered if he was psychic, too. She didn't give me all the details, but long story short, they did get married, and he took her back to America with him.

Bea started explaining that my mother and father were standing right next to me. They were there and wanted to give me messages. She talked to them and would nod her head and laugh at times. She interacted with them as if they were living. She gave names of living people, too. She asked who Tony was, and I said I had an Uncle Tony. She said it was good for me to keep in contact with him. I had to agree!

One other name that came up was Franny. Yes, my sister-in-law. She had a message for Franny from her mother! Her mother wanted to give her some messages directly. She didn't want to tell me so I couldn't tell Franny. Bea asked for Franny to get her own reading with her. Well, that was it! A one-on-one medium reading for Franny was the other way her deceased parents were going to connect with Franny! Once again, I was indirectly involved with Franny and her deceased parents. Franny did end up going to see Bea and was quite impressed. That is pretty amazing since Franny is quite the skeptic. Franny's parents choose wisely. Bea didn't disappoint. The messages for the future she gave me did eventually come true. Her percentage of accuracy was quite high. Pat agreed, too.

A few years later, Franny had "Pat the Medium," as we called her, come to her house for a party. It was impressive for Franny to let her skeptic guard down. Bea had softened her up a bit. What also helped Franny open up was that the medium came highly recommended. Some family and friends were in attendance. Like I said, we just loved this stuff! Franny was read first and came out amazed. I thought it was a very good indication. However, Pat was read before me and complained that Pat the Medium talked more about my sister's friend than she did about her! That was unusual for my sister. In time, we figured out why.

I was hoping to connect with my Uncle Tony, who had passed away earlier in the year. We had made a pact. I said he had to promise me that after he passed away, he would come through in a medium reading. This way, it would be proof to me there was life beyond death. It would also show communication was still possible, even after death.

Pat the Medium first connected me with my father. He brought along our dog that he used to walk all the time. He showed himself to Pat, walking the dog. My father really did love animals. My father brought my mother with him. Pat the Medium explained that my father was a more grounded soul, a protector, and had a better connection with the physical realm. My mother did not and was wispier. She was more connected to the spiritual realm. Pat the Medium told me that if I felt someone lightly touching my hair, it was my mother.

Pat the Medium asked if I knew a man who served his country. She told me my father was bringing him through and they were close in life. It was good old Uncle Tony! He didn't disappoint and held his promise! Pat the Medium related that Uncle Tony said to give me the message, "I'm here! I'm here! I made it! Yes, they accepted me in heaven! Can you believe it?" He was quite a character, and back in his younger years, you could have called him a rascal. I'm assuming the pearly gates looked at his whole life and let him in! I couldn't have been happier! I loved the validation, and it made me even more of a believer.

What she told me next, though, was a shocker! I didn't know if I could believe it. She said I had read about Edgar Cayce and was fascinated with what he could do. Yes, that was true, and I confirmed it for her. Then she said I would be able to do what he did. Now I started disbelieving! Was she crazy? Edgar Cayce could go into a trance and was able to give people information. She said I would be able to go into a trance-like state and connect with people who had passed away.

Pat the Medium also said Metatron was surrounding me. I had no clue who Metatron was . . . maybe a Transformer? You know, from the movie? I later looked it up; Megatron was from the *Transformers* movie. Metatron is an Archangel and helps with writing. He can also be referred to as "messenger from God." I was thinking to myself, *my sister is right*. We can't be sure if this woman really knows what she's talking about.

Pat the Medium went on to say that the woman, Carol, who used to read my tarot cards, wanted me to start learning how to read the tarot cards. Sadly, Carol had passed away from lymphoma. Pat the Medium explained that Carol said she would help me learn and was excited for me. She said I just had to believe. I will tell you more about Carol later.

Chapter 4
Revelation

I don't know if it was actually Carol's doing, but less than a year later, an opportunity presented itself. My friend and I used to attend different classes and events at a holistic center. A new class was being offered, *Learn to Read Tarot Cards*. A thought immediately popped into my head to go and check it out. I asked my friend if she wanted to come with me, but she could not, so off I went alone. I felt Carol had sent me the thought and possibly some courage vibes, too. I walked into class quite open-minded and very willing to learn.

One thing that is absolutely crucial for you to know about me: I love to learn! Certain topics appeal to me more than others, but I am a seeker of knowledge. School was always a place I looked forward to going. Don't get me wrong; I felt some classes were truly a waste of time. My favorite ones, though, took me to places where I could explore and excel. I know it's cliché, but knowledge is power. I soaked up the lessons, swelled with eager confidence, and was emblazed with a new understanding to be used in battle. No violence was involved — only determination to make my life and those around me better.

Let's get back to the tarot card class. The teacher, Jessica McKay, was a tarot card reader herself and emphasized not to get caught up in the written meanings of the cards. Googling the meaning of the cards was forbidden. She wanted us to focus on what the cards meant to each and every one of us. She wanted us to use our own intuition to take over and not use someone else's interpretation. I guess you can compare it to the concept of the dreamer who needs to interpret his or her own dream. It's best not to look it up in a dream book that is subject to the author's interpretation.

I will shout it to the rooftops! In my opinion, this method of reading the tarot cards is the BEST EVER! It allows you to flex your intuitive muscles and come up with your interpretation. It gives you strength and courage to realize your potential — in essence, your "gift." Thank you, Jessica, for allowing our class to take flight and soar into the mystical, magical world of unleashing our intuition through tarot card reading. I am forever grateful to you and your methodology.

We were asked to pick a deck of tarot cards that "resonated" with us. I picked the Norbert Losche Cosmic Tarot deck. To be perfectly honest, I gravitated to them because the pictures were so beautiful. To me, each card looked like a perfect work of art to be admired. When I held them in my hands, they just felt right.

We were instructed to get in groups of two, preferably with a stranger. Always being the good student, I listened to my teacher. After some explanations from Jessica, we were ready to begin. I went first to read a woman I had never seen before. I looked at the cards she had picked and took some time to see what popped in my head. A story started to form about her son.

I must be perfectly honest; I thought I was making the whole thing up. I spoke to her about a son and how she needed to help him more than her daughter. Her daughter was the stronger of her two children and resented that the mother coddled her son. Her daughter didn't speak to her son, and that caused a great rift between mother and daughter. These words seemed to flow right out of my mouth. I was waiting for the woman to look at me and say, "What the hell are you talking about?" Instead, she looked at me and burst into tears.

After she composed herself, she said I was right about the whole situation. When she told me that, I was stunned!

I couldn't believe the "story" was true! I thought it was just my imagination, but in fact, it was my intuition. She gave me validation.

I felt like a kid who thinks her dad is still holding on to the bike while she's riding, but realizes she is doing it all by herself. I felt the exhilaration of having that encompassing sensation; I was hooked. There was no going back. I just knew this was something I loved to do, and more importantly, had the capability. The song lyrics, "I've got the power" echoed in my head!

Chapter 5
Practice Is A Must

What did I do next? I focused on the tarot cards and practiced, practiced, practiced. Who were my recipients? My family, of course! The women in my family and my husband's family also loved this stuff and were eager to be read. My sister, sisters-in-law, niece, her twin girls, my cousin, a longtime friend of the family my sons call "aunt," and my mother-in-law were all part of the entourage. There was one lone male, my nephew Bryan, who just loves having his cards read. Family gatherings were the hot spot for me to take out my cards, and they would line up to be read. It was a true win-win for us all! I must share with you how I truly love the win-win situation! When both parties are happy, that balance is extremely satisfying. If you strive for it in life, it will be quite rewarding. Hey, just a little philosophical note to ponder!

Sometimes when doing a reading, something comes up that makes you really uncomfortable and challenges your moral compass. This happened to me when I read for Bryan's partner, Bob*. Bob was open-minded about this stuff, but he was a very private person. He wasn't one to talk a lot, unlike Bryan, who loves people and, even more so, loves talking to them. I guess they balanced one another; opposites attract. This was the case for them both, even physically. Bryan is tall and thin; Bob is short and stout.

One day, I stopped by their house to do a tarot card reading for Bob. Bryan went out for a walk to give us privacy. Now mind you, I was still new to this stuff. I hadn't been practicing all that long and still had some doubts about my abilities. Nonetheless, I had Bob shuffle the deck, and the process began. I started to read the five cards he picked and almost choked, both figuratively and literally. I saw another man in the cards. I felt strongly that Bryan didn't know about this man, and Bob was happy to keep it that way.

It was a predicament for me. What do I do? Do I say what I actually see, or just say, "Hey, why don't you shuffle the cards again?" It's like seeing your friend's husband with another woman. Do you say something to your friend or not? I chose the latter. I didn't say a word to Bryan about the cards.

I told Bob I saw another man close to him and he had a decision to make; stay with my nephew or choose the other man. The other man had money around him. I was honest with Bob and told him I was not going to say anything to Bryan about what came up in the cards. I was hoping the partner would ditch the other guy and stay with Bryan. Bryan would stay in ignorant bliss, and no one would be the wiser.

Also, my moral compass guided me to do the right thing. Whenever I do a reading, I hold complete confidence. I don't "spill the beans" to anyone. If the person I'm reading wants to do that, it is his or her choice to make, not mine.

Can you guess what happened a week later? I didn't see it coming. Maybe my intuition was out to lunch that day, or maybe it just wasn't meant for me to know. Perhaps it was meant for me to savor the surprise. My sister-in-law, Franny, my nephew's mom, called me and said Bob had broken up with Bryan. She said she just couldn't believe it!

I almost fell off my chair! My heart went out to Bryan, yet it was proof to me that I was right about the tarot cards! There was a validation staring me in the face. No denying it! Bob DID have another man, the one with the money, and chose him instead of Bryan. Bryan was devastated. His heart was truly broken, and he kept saying he never saw it coming. When Bryan asked Bob if there was someone else, he immediately said no. I wasn't going to be the one to burst his bubble.

This sad story, in a strange twist of fate, encouraged me to continue with my tarot readings. Unfortunately, for Bryan, his misfortune became my fortune. My reading became a cruel reality.

Practicing tarot card reading heightened my intuition. One message I heard loud and clear was that my brother-in-law, Sal, should also practice the tarot cards because he definitely had a "gift." I shared this message with him and, at first, he didn't believe it. To prove it to him, I bought him the same tarot card deck I have. Once he got them, I convinced him to practice, and he started doing readings for our family. I asked him to read me and let me tell you; he was excellent! Whatever he said was spot on with what was happening.

He liked reading his cards with past, present, and future. His technique was different than mine. This is wonderful since each person who is interested should find what works well for him or her. Like painting or any other interest, find your own style. He did and he excelled! I didn't actually teach him, just exposed him to it, and he soared. Pat was quite supportive of him since she also "just knew" he was capable.

Chapter 6
My Sister Pat

We need to focus on my sister now. As I said previously, Pat could see and dream of dead people. She had phenomenal intuition, and many people would seek her out for advice. Pat was a straight-shooter, a tell-it-like-it-is person. Everyone loved her for it, even though sometimes the truth stings. Throw in her excellent sense of humor, and she was someone you just wanted to be around. People enjoyed her company for different reasons and on many levels. She helped so many and never looked for anything in return. A jealous bone could not be found in her body. Pat was always ready to give her love freely. I felt special because she was my sister.

When leukemia struck her out of the blue, there was no doubt in my mind, nor in anyone else's, she would slay it. Pat was strong-willed, a rebel all her life. Nothing was going to beat her down. When the doctors were optimistic about their aggressive methods of attack, Pat was all in. Our family was there to support her however we could.

Round one of chemo was a dirty fighter. Along with some common side effects like hair loss and nausea, it hit below the belt with a wretched red rash all over her body. That didn't deter my sister. She still came out swinging. Not only did Pat have her family's support, but that of the nursing staff at Columbia Presbyterian Hospital. These men and women had angel's wings. The love they mixed in with tending to their patients was from another dimension. A few of Pat's team of doctors could be described that way as well.

When Sal and I would visit Pat, we tried out our newfound interest in tarot card reading on the nursing staff. The days were long and sometimes monotonous in the hospital. It gave Pat pleasure to watch us do readings for her angels. Occasionally, she would say something to enhance it. Pat had the ability but chose not to practice it. She preferred to use her humor as a gift to them while leaving the readings to Sal and me. Word spread, and we read for even more of the staff.

The doctors suggested a bone marrow transplant for Pat. Billy and I eagerly took a test to see if we were candidates. Unfortunately, neither of us were. Surprisingly, strangers were a better match than siblings. How can a stranger be a better match than a blood relative? The doctor explained this phenomenon, but to this day, I still don't understand.

Pat was able to go home for a short time. She was able to do some of her favorite things, like shopping and visiting friends and family. The highlight was celebrating Billy's birthday with laughs and the usual enormous amount of food. What do you expect from a typical Italian family? Of course, Sal and I read tarot cards for some family members. Pat did not want hers read at the time. She didn't want to go back to the hospital either. Her fighting spirit had changed. She told her daughter, Danielle that if she got another round of chemo, it was going to kill her.

Reluctantly, though, Pat went back. This time she was put in an older section of the hospital where the atmosphere was depressingly bleak. Pat's attitude and body deteriorated. Her familiar angels did not work in that section. She pleaded with one of the doctors to let her go back to the special wing. This doctor slashed Pat with his curt word, "No!" Fortunately, he was one bad apple among the shiny, crisp compassionate ones. The head doctor transferred Pat back to her angelic atmosphere. Sal quit his part-time job and stayed at the hospital with her 24/7. He was truly devoted to his wife, and Pat was truly appreciative. I visited one or two times a week, as did Danielle, our nephew Bryan, our cousin Liz, Billy and Franny, and Sal's niece, Joanie. Other relatives visited when they could. Family surrounded Pat, which made her feel better. Her hope of coming home for Thanksgiving allowed her to linger in joyfulness.

Thanksgiving is a very special holiday for our family. All of us are together at my house, unlike Christmas, where my husband, children, and I spend it with my husband's side of the family. We truly bond, eat too much, play right-left-center, look at old pictures, and we each say what we are thankful for at the dinner table.

To get the essence of Pat's humor, I have to tell you about what happened on Thanksgiving in 2007. Pat topped herself with what she was thankful for. Remember my cousin Theresa, the one who had the dream about our grandmother dying? To give you some more background on her, she was never married. I always told her, though, one day she would. I just *knew*, even before I learned to read the tarot cards.

Theresa went to her fiftieth high school reunion. She started talking to a guy she used to date in high school. He had flown up from Florida, where he lived, to attend. They ended up having a long-distance relationship. Long story short, Theresa was a first time, beautiful, blushing bride at the age of sixty-eight! Now mind you, Theresa was an old-fashioned kind of gal and quite religious.

Getting back to Pat, she announced at the dinner table to our entire family, "I am thankful that my cousin, Theresa, finally got laid!" We were all just hysterical! Some of us were laughing so hard we started crying! You see, not only did we want Pat to be well enough to come home from the hospital and spend Thanksgiving with the family, we were all looking forward to cracking up about the funny thing she would say she was thankful for.

Unfortunately, Pat's immune system was not strong enough, and she had to stay in the hospital for Thanksgiving. She had also been filling up with fluids. Still, her doctors were encouraging. Pat's mental health seemed better, and although disappointed about Thanksgiving, she was looking forward to Christmas. Sal and I continued to read tarot cards for the nurses. One reading we did for Pat showed that she was moving. She did want to move from her shore house and wanted to live at the same fifty-five and over community where Billy and Franny lived.

While Pat was in the hospital, a surprise visitor came to see her. Remember the story about my mother not speaking to her relatives? Pat and her son, Bobby, had a falling out. Issues had been building for some time, but the straw that broke the camel's back was related to his daughter, Dana. Pat adored her first grandchild and they had a special bond. Dana squealed with delight whenever she saw her grandmother and thoroughly loved being with her. Pat and Sal would sometimes babysit for Dana. Details of their differences will not be discussed here, best to keep this family matter private. Sadly, Bobby and Pat did not speak for fifteen years.

Have you guessed the surprise visitor? It was Bobby, her son. He actually came to the hospital to see his mother. Did they make up? He told her he loved her, but she kept her eyes closed. Was she sleeping? Did she forgive him? No one knows because my sister could barely speak.

What I do know, based on my just *knowing* capability, was that my sister needed to see her granddaughter. Dana was going to college at the time and came home for Thanksgiving. She was supposed to see Pat, but unfortunately, it fell through.

Pat's condition worsened with the fluid build-up, so the doctors decided to operate on her. After the operation, her condition plummeted. She became so weak; she could hardly eat, drink, or speak. It was a shock to the entire family. We, as well as the doctors, had been so hopeful and so positive.

One night, I had a dream about my deceased father. In the dream, I was at Billy and Franny's house. I saw my father, and he was all red. It was as if he was being electrified and sparks flew wildly around him. His body kept writhing in pain. He kept losing his balance and falling. He would try to stand up and withstand the torture. I was crying hysterically and said, "Daddy, please, please don't fight it anymore. You are trying so hard to take it, but please, you don't have to. Please let it go. Please don't be tortured anymore, I beg of you." I saw Billy and Franny walk in the door. They had just returned from seeing Pat in the hospital. That was the end of my dream.

My interpretation of the dream was that my father was representing my sister. The chemo, as she had predicted, was killing her. She tried to endure it. I believe she didn't want to leave her family. In my heart, I didn't want her to suffer anymore. My deceased father, from beyond, was showing me what was happening to her. He allowed me to feel my emotions about it and probably prepare me for what was going to happen.

I told some of my relatives about the dream, and they had various interpretations. Not one of them thought it represented Pat dying. I "just knew" from my dream that she was dying. Shortly afterward, Pat asked Sal why her deceased mother was at the foot of her bed. She also said she saw Sal's deceased brother and wondered why he was there. Those sightings solidified to me that her time was near. As you may know, it is quite common for people near death to start seeing people who have passed away. I have read and do believe that deceased loved ones come for the person to make their transition easier.

Shortly after Pat's operation to clear the fluid in her lungs, the doctors concluded, to their dismay, that she *was*, in fact, dying. Hospice was to take over. It was a wretched, gut-wrenching shock, especially since the doctors had been so hopeful and encouraging. Our family just couldn't believe it.

Even though I *knew*, somehow, I still had hope. I could have been wrong about my dream, but to hear those words was cruelly devastating. When he got home from work, I told my husband, Mitch, and I just sobbed uncontrollably. He held on to me tight and cried, too. My son, Sean, came into the room. He hugged us both and started crying. It is difficult for Sean to share his emotions with us. The news broke a barrier for him; we all connected our grief with comfort for one another.

I was an adjunct professor at the time, and finals were right around the corner. I got coverage for my class and went to see Pat more often, not knowing which day would be her last. She could hardly eat or speak. Sleeping was her primary state, although one day she shocked us! Sal, Danielle, Billy, Franny, and I were at Pat's bedside. Pat sat straight up in bed and said, "Get me out of here! I want to go home!" She was her feisty, old self again and hopping mad!

Sal replied, "Ok, Pat, I'll go and get the car."

Billy joked, "How about I get you a rope and hoist you out the window. We can spring you out of here!"

My sister and the rest of us all had a good laugh. Pat was smiling and seemed really happy. I thought it was a miracle! Pat was on the mend! She found her strength and was getting better! A few minutes passed, and sadly, she lay back down to fall fast asleep. Her time was coming quickly. Another common occurrence when a person is close to death: they rally. For some reason, they very briefly get better before they get worse. Pat never spoke again.

Pat had been waiting for her granddaughter, Dana, to come and see her. Dana would be getting out of college for winter break. The days went by, but no Dana. I knew Pat had very little time left. I knew she was hanging on to the hope of seeing her beloved Dana. Their bond, even through all the turmoil, could not be broken. However, there was no word on exactly when Dana would be able to see her grandmother.

I planned on driving to see Pat the day after the "miracle." As I started driving, I had thoughts about whether or not I should just stop at Bobby's house to see if Dana was home. I was thinking that if Dana was home from college, she could drive with me to see Pat. I was torn, though, wondering if it was my place to do this. I asked for a sign, something to show me if I should drive to Bobby's house.

About ten seconds later, as I was driving, I looked to my left.

There was a billboard that read YES in huge letters. It was an ad for insurance. I had driven that way to see Pat so many times before and never noticed it. If that wasn't a *sign*, I do not know what was!

That was it for me. I drove straight to Bobby's house. My adrenalin was soaring, and I felt like I was on a mission from God — literally! I had no qualms about going right up to the door and ringing the bell. Mind you, no one knew I was coming. There were unknowns. Was Dana home? Would anyone be home? Would anyone answer the door? I had to find out, and there was no stopping me!

Bobby's wife, Kristin, answered, and a sense of peace came over me. All my worrying thoughts about past history fell by the wayside. I calmly asked if I could take Dana with me to see her grandmother. I said I was on my way, and it was no trouble for me at all to bring Dana. She said Dana was still at college and wouldn't be home until late that night.

My heart sank hearing those leaden words. I tearfully said that Pat was dying, and I knew she was holding on to see Dana. I begged her to please let Dana see her grandmother. I knew Pat's end was very near, a matter of hours or possibly a day or two. I was respectful and appealed to the greater good. She promised that once Dana got home, she and Bobby would drive her to the hospital to see Pat. I felt so relieved and happy. I just knew this was Pat's dying wish.

I ran to my car and sped off to the hospital. Sal was there when I got to Pat's room. He was such a good husband, never leaving her side. He showed his devotion in so many ways, sleeping on a lounge chair in her room, eating here and there, playing music to soothe her. I told him to take a break and get some coffee.

I was alone in the room with my sister. I couldn't contain my enthusiasm! I whispered to her, "Pat, guess what!" I always liked to have her guess things. She would say "What?" in like a "You're a pain in the ass" type of response. Although I felt she actually enjoyed this banter, I could have been kidding myself.

Pat couldn't answer this time, since her voice had left her. I said, "Dana is coming to see you!" Her eyes popped open! I was so happy to see her response. I told her about going to the house and let her know that Dana was still in college and coming home that night. I wanted her to know that Dana hadn't come to see her yet because she had still been at college. My sister smiled.

I spent the day with Pat, Sal, Danielle, and her husband, Phil. Danielle was by Pat's side all through this whole ordeal. They had such a strong bond, like my mother and I had. They were best friends, and it tore Danielle apart to see her mother this way and know in a flash she would be gone. It was truly heart-wrenching. Danielle admitted to feeling guilty that she made Pat have the chemo again, but what choice did she have? She wanted her mother alive, and that seemed like the best option at the time. It was her only option.

The day passed and it was time for me to leave. I went to say good-bye to my sister, who I thought was sleeping. I held her hand and said, "Bye Pat, I'm going home now." She opened her eyes and I saw such love in them. It's amazing when speech leaves, eyes can be even more expressive. Shakespeare, one of my very favorite authors, was right. "The eyes are the window to your soul." Pat started to cry; tears rolled down her soft cheeks. She pursed her lips. Danielle was sitting next to her and said to me, "She is giving you a kiss." I didn't understand at first. I was shocked she was able to make that gesture. I kissed her and was crying, too.

The thought occurred to me that this would be the last time I would see my sister. Pat then mouthed, "I love you." I was utterly amazed at this; it was like a miracle that she had the strength and desire to do this. I was crying and told her I loved her, too. I hugged her tight, not ever wanting to let her go, but I knew I had to. I looked at Sal, Danielle, and Phil, then gazed at Pat. Sal walked me out the door.

I cried uncontrollably. I kept saying I couldn't believe she was able to do that. Pat gave me a gift that I will keep with me throughout my life. In my heart, I felt she was forever grateful for what I did to arrange for Dana to see her. The grace of God allowed it. I told Sal I knew this was the last goodbye. I think Pat knew, too, and that is also why she did what she did. It was so important to her to let me know she loved me.

I kept texting Dana's mother, Kristin, to check if Dana was still going to see Pat. She said it would be hard to go that night after such a long day for Dana. I pleaded with her to go that night, no matter how late. I did not know how much longer Pat would last; the window was rapidly shrinking.

Dana *did* go to see her grandmother that Saturday night. I will be forever thankful to Bobby and Kristin. They managed to bring Dana there, even though it was late. Dana went in by herself to see her grandmother. She told me that Pat held her hand tight. I'm guessing she didn't want to let it go. Maybe she wanted to infuse her love and have Dana keep it with her. There had been too much time lost for them not to be able to spend time together and share their loving bond. In the end, God allowed them to reconnect. Pat's wish came true.

Early Monday morning, Sal woke up to the song *Time to Say Goodbye* by Andrea Bocelli. A nurse walked in, checked on Pat, and shook her head. Sal knew what she meant. I got his call on December 21, the opposite number of Pat's birthday on May 12. I feel that Pat held on until she was able to see Dana. I have heard many stories about people who wait to see certain loved ones before they die. Once they have done so, perhaps they are more comfortable to leave. I believe Pat left peacefully because my mother, father, grandmother, and other deceased relatives were there to comfort her and take her home. Yes, the tarot cards were right; she did move to a new home. The dream I had involving my father also played out. My sister's eerie prediction of the chemo killing her became a reality. Pat released herself from the pain and suffering in the physical world.

Since then, I have had many dreams about Pat. Some of them were actually "visit" dreams. That's where you feel you are truly with the deceased person again. The dream is very clear and you can easily remember it. I love the feeling of touching, hugging, and talking with her. My belief is that we are truly together, just in another realm.

I have done readings for myself where Pat has connected with me. She has given me plenty of messages about myself and my family. I am grateful that she continues to give me guidance.

Two years after Pat passed, she "shocked the shit out of me!" These were words she would have used to describe what happened, not mine. Pat certainly had a way with words to make an impact! I guess it took her that long to develop enough skill and energy to do what she did.

I must tell you about this strange occurrence. I was texting Franny and Sal about going out to lunch for Danielle's birthday. We were going back and forth with texts. I looked down at the text and couldn't believe my eyes! There was a text that appeared to have been sent by me. It was on my side of the screen. It read: "I can possibly go on Thursday. Let me know where and what time. Ask Liz, too. She will go."

Now at the time, remember, Pat had been gone for a little over two years. My cousin, Liz, had unexpectedly passed away from a heart attack only two months prior to this text. Pat and Liz were very close and did lots of things together . . . two peas in a pod.

I definitely did not type that text message. It just appeared! I stared at it in disbelief! How could that be? I still don't have a rational explanation for it. If you or anyone you know does, please contact me. My rationale is that Pat somehow got that text message through. When she was alive, she would have sent that message. Pat is no longer physically with us, but I guess that didn't stop her. She wanted to be included in going out to lunch to celebrate her daughter's birthday. Pat is still connected! It made perfect sense that she would want Liz to join us!

Pat has been gone now for five years. Recently, she used my phone again, but in a different way. One day, I was feeling kind of lonely. I decided to do some work on my computer to keep busy and had my cell phone next to me. I was quite involved with what I was doing when the sound of my phone startled me. It wasn't the sound of it ringing; it was the sound of it dialing! However, both of my hands were on the computer. I kid you not; my phone was dialing all by itself. I looked down, and guess who was dialing? My sister! I had kept her phone number on my phone, and as I looked down, her name, Pat, appeared. Logic got the better of me, and I quickly hung up the phone. I rationalized, someone else must have that number now, and I did not want to speak with them. If my psychic side won out, I would have remained on the line to see who it was, with the expectation it would be Pat. If this ever happens again, I will wait to see who actually does answer. If it is Pat, it will be more proof to me that our loved ones live on and use different methods to connect. In my soul, I know this is true. My explanation for why she had the phone call me reminds me of the song I associate with her, *Ain't No Mountain High Enough* by Diana Ross, and the lyrics, "If you need me, call me." Pat first sent this song to her daughter, Danielle, when she was feeling sad. Danielle told me about it, and we decided that was Pat's "song" as a sign from her.

If Pat was still living and I was lonely, I would call her like I had done countless times before. She knew I would not do that currently, but I feel she wanted me to know she was there for me. She knew I needed her, and yes, her love for me is still alive. I feel that's why the phone started dialing; she wanted me to call her. She wanted me to know that she was there for me when I really needed her. That's my explanation; you may come to a different conclusion. Please take a little time to ponder this.

Pat was an amazing person in life and still is now, in another dimension. Her psychic abilities were to be admired throughout her life and she has shown me that her abilities continue in the afterlife.

Chapter 7
Influential People

I wanted to expand my psychic abilities and learn more. I took a psychic class with psychic medium Artie Hoffman, who had previously read me. I thought he was excellent with his readings and was eager to take a class with him. In his class, though, we didn't read tarot cards. We had to pair up with someone and just say what came to mind about that person. Guess who I was paired up with? Artie!

I was petrified to read him because he was not only the instructor, he was well known. I was intimidated, but he was very gracious and encouraging. He soothed me enough to allow my stress level to diminish. I relaxed, and words just came flowing out. To my delight, he validated that what I said was true! Wow! I couldn't believe I was reading the gifted reader! My confidence level shot up and I must credit Artie. Without his support, I wouldn't have been able to read him. He also built up my confidence to read for others. He helped me believe in myself. The force of my belief within manifested itself and empowered me. I am forever grateful.

My friend, Penelope*, also loves to help others. She **believes** helping people is one of her strengths. I can't agree more, and many people feel the same way about Penelope. One day she saw a stranded family on the side of the highway. It was really hot out, so she stopped and gave them some food and water. She stayed until the police came and didn't leave until everything was under control. Another time, while driving, Penelope saw a woman lying on the ground. There was no one else around her.

She immediately stopped the car and ran over to help her. The woman told her she had just fallen. I can go on and on to tell you the countless stories of her altruism.

We have discussed the idea of her always seeming to be in the right place when someone truly needs help. She is not like most people who just keep walking. Penelope immediately goes into help mode, and the strangers are forever grateful. She and her family also organize drives for people affected by hurricanes and disasters. Penelope contacts her community, and people come in droves, dropping off all kinds of clothes, food, and supplies. She arranges for a tractor-trailer to collect the donated materials and distribute them to those in need.

There are countless times when Penelope does random acts of kindness. She recently started a kindness foundation. I truly admire her selflessness and love for others. She understands the great importance of connectivity and belief.

Our friendship started out in an unusual way. We met at a local function in town since our sons are close in age. However, she didn't live in my town where the function was being held; her cousin, Chris, did. Penelope and her son went with Chris and her son. We all started talking and seemed to get along well. I asked them if they would like to come for a swim at my house the following week. Chris could not, but Penelope could.

The following week Penelope and her son came over and we started talking. We realized fairly quickly that there was one thing in particular that was near and dear to both of us — mediums. Penelope told me that she and her mother had been read by the famous and fabulous John Edward, although he wasn't famous at the time they were read. He connected with Penelope's father and as a result, Penelope's mother had a new outlook on life. Her deceased husband's words gave her courage, so to speak, to come alive again. Penelope and her mom are forever grateful to the amazing John Edward. I am in awe of him and his abilities. I watched his shows, saw him in person with Penelope, and read all his books. John Edward is a role model for all, on so many levels. He is a truly genuine and gifted medium with a humbleness to be greatly admired.

Penelope and I went to see two more icons, Sylvia Browne, God rest her soul, and Long Island Medium, Theresa Caputo. I have read each of their books that describe their abilities and experiences. They are excellent teachers. I also want to mention my appreciation for their humor, each unique and so entertaining. I have great respect for them both.

More recently, Penelope and I went to see the Hollywood Medium, Tyler Henry, in Atlantic City. We both love his TV shows. He's so adorable, you just want to squeeze him. Tyler Henry's compassion is exquisite. You are mesmerized into wanting to be drawn into his arms for a warm milk hug. I greatly admire his amazing mediumship abilities and his embodiment of a kind, funny, caring, and loving young man with an old soul.

However, I do have a favorite psychic who was not famous . . . Carol, whom I mentioned previously. Carol is my favorite, but not because she was 100 percent accurate. There were a few things that were off the mark. Remember my free will theory I wrote about earlier? Don't get me wrong; she was spot on for numerous things. For example, she told me I would get a job that I'd have for a little while, but it would be a stepping stone to something else. I felt this message was related to my job as an adjunct professor. The skills I used there allowed me to teach intuitive classes and feel comfortable speaking in front of people. Carol also told me to expand my intuitive abilities through various methods, which would serve me well in the future. I took a variety of intuitive classes and read numerous books about the subject. My education regarding intuition is certainly serving me well! Carol also spoke about my husband who, at the time, had changed jobs a couple times. She said he would settle into a job and stay for a long time, which would serve him very well. My husband has been in his current job for thirteen years, he is highly regarded for his role in the company, and still going strong! Those three examples of Carol's predictions truly became realities.

Carol had a completely true desire to help others. She cared for her clients and wanted to give guidance. She also had a great sense of humor, which I adored, and we laughed plenty of times during every reading. Her personality drew you in, and for your time spent with her, you were captivated. We still have a relationship, even though she has passed away, and I do miss her! I was meditating one day, and she gave me a message: "You aren't getting rid of me any time soon!" She relayed that she would help me with my tarot card readings. She always wanted to help. Thankfully, some things never change! Carol was the essence of a woman beautiful both inside and out. I will be forever grateful for her beauty and caring guidance.

Penelope was also read by Carol. She was very impressed and loved her, too. Although not all, but most of the things Carol told her came true. For example, Carol told Penelope she would be moving by water and also very close to a school. At the time, it did not make sense because Penelope had no plans for moving. Eventually, Penelope did both; she purchased two different houses. One was near water, and the other was near a school, just like Carol said. Carol had told her the move would be good in more ways than one. Penelope can definitely vouch for that! Penelope and I speak about Carol from time to time, and it always puts a smile on our faces.

Carol was a professional psychic. I want to introduce you to my college roommate, Daisy*, someone who has a totally different profession, one in finance, and who I feel has great intuition. During the time Pat was in the hospital, Daisy contacted two of our college friends and me. Daisy had moved to California after college, and it had been many years since we had seen one another. She wanted to get together and meet at her new vacation home in Upstate New York. It was much closer to New Jersey than California! She had purchased a barn with lots of land and converted it into an amazing home. Quite the feat!

I was excited to see Daisy, and for fun, I brought along the tarot cards. I read for her, her husband, daughter, and our college friends. They all got a hoot out of it and we enjoyed our time together catching up.

A few months later, Daisy had an important decision to make. She called me and asked if I would read the cards to help with her decision. I was still not fully confident about my abilities and made it perfectly clear. Daisy insisted that things came true for her and her family. She was confident that I had the ability. I agreed to read the cards, which did point her in a particular direction. She got in touch with me a few months later to let me know she made her choice and things were working out well. She thanked me for my *intuitive* guidance.

I hadn't heard from Daisy in a couple years. In 2017, she decided to have a vow renewal party for being married thirty years. The party was going to be hosted at her vacation home. She wanted me to be part of the entertainment by reading tarot cards and was inviting about seventy people! Again, I was hesitant, not knowing if I would feel comfortable. She assured me I would do just great. I asked if Sal could also come to read. There were so many people! She happily agreed.

The night of the party came and I was nervous, yet excited. Sal had the same feeling. My husband was quite supportive, even knowing I would be busy for a while. He looked forward to meeting new people and sharing stories.

I was put in what looked like a teepee. A Native American theme set the atmosphere. Sal was in an area quite a bit away from me, next to a cart filled with flowers. An announcement was made that the tarot card readers were ready to begin. People lined up and before I knew it, I was reading with confidence and grace. I felt compassion for the people and told them what I heard and saw in the cards. The majority of guests were quite pleased with their readings. I felt exhilarated to give them information they needed to hear.

One man in particular got an unusual reading. I told him about present and future happenings. Then I felt something different. A presence came over me. I asked if there was a woman that passed away who was close to him. Up until then, I normally did not get mediumship abilities while reading cards. However, through the cards, I was able to connect with this man's loved one, who turned out to be his mother. She had passed when he was only a young boy. I told him I felt her presence and she, in fact, had messages. He looked unsure, gazing at me with apprehension.

I told him his mother was always around him and was so very proud of what he accomplished in his life. She saw him as a man of dignity and compassion. She admired him as a successful businessman and a caring partner; she couldn't have been prouder. After hearing these words, he broke out sobbing. He told me his aunt and uncle had raised him, and though they loved him like their own son, he sought the love of his mother. She had an abundance of it to give, and gave her approval of how he lived his life. If I had handed him a million dollars instead of giving him those words from his mother, I feel it would have paled in comparison. Her gift was priceless and so full of love. Right before my eyes, I saw the vastness, expansion, and healing power of love. The man floated away with contentment and sheer peace.

There were no further connections with the dead for the rest of the night. A mother knew the depth of her son's need and crossed all boundaries to fill him with her love. That reading still holds a special place in my heart and certainly in his.

I must have read over twenty people that night. They just kept coming and amazingly, I didn't feel exhausted. I usually go to sleep around 9 or 9:30 PM, but I was fueled up with exhilaration that kept my energy going strong. The line kept getting longer, but people waited patiently and chatted with friends. The idea that I could actually do this was proven to me over and over during that night. It was just what I needed to prove to myself that I did, in fact, have the ability or *gift*.

However, there was one young woman who didn't seem to be a believer. It was as though she wanted to prove me wrong with almost everything I said. I lost my clarity, or maybe it was my confidence, at one point during the reading, and she became triumphant. I got the feeling that was her mission all along. I retreated and didn't have much more to tell her after that.

Upon reflection later that night, I realized I couldn't help everyone. I concluded that, for those who accept my help and guidance, I am at peace. For those who don't believe that I want to help, I must accept their beliefs and be at peace. This is not an easy lesson for me to learn. I am a people pleaser.

The next day we went to Daisy's house for a BBQ. Sal and I were not scheduled to do any readings. Well, you guessed it, we ended up reading people we hadn't seen the night before. Favorable words of our abilities had spread. We ended up reading for another three hours. Again, our energies were fueled by the desires of others. Some were curious, then came to realizations. Others had questions and needed to find answers.

I am grateful to Daisy. She believed in my ability. She gave me an audience and an atmosphere that proved to me what she already knew. My true calling in life is to help others. My newfound way of doing that is through tarot card reading and mediumship. She shared my gift with people in her life who gave her gifts of all different kinds. The cycle lives on.

My two college friends, Caroline and Debbie, also attended Daisy's party. They both live in New Jersey. Remember, Caroline is the one my mother adored. We all get together about two to three times a year. Each time we meet at Rutgers for lunch, I bring my tarot cards and read them. Sometimes one or two other women who went to college with us also join us and I read them, too. We have a good time with it.

I adore Caroline like my mother did. Caroline has a great sense of humor and loves to tease me. At one of our Rutgers lunches, she said she wanted to read my cards. "How hard can it be?" she teased. Well, we just cracked up with the "reading" she gave me. It was all in good fun.

"I knew from the first day I met you at college, you were strange," Caroline good-naturedly said, "although I must admit, you do seem to have a knack for this. Pursue tarot card and medium readings — it's more fun than accounting and financial literacy!" All these years, I sought Caroline out when I wanted her opinion. She hasn't steered me wrong yet! Once again, I'm following her advice. Thanks, Caroline!

Have you noticed that some of my friends also have good intuition and psychic ability? You know what they say about "birds of a feather!" My friend Bonnie, who I have known the longest, is very psychic! I have known her since our sophomore year in high school. When I met her, we didn't discuss our psychic abilities. That was revealed later in our friendship, although Bonnie's mom's psychic abilities presented themselves early on. She "just knew" about different things. I enjoyed asking her about boys I dated, and she was always on target with Bonnie's love interests, too. My friend inherited her mom's talent. She didn't need tarot cards to bring out information.

Through the years, as friends do, we would discuss each other's problems. We would give each other advice, but it seemed to come from a *knowing.* Bonnie was right most of the time. It is funny how we hit it off immediately when we met in high school. I'm guessing our souls were familiar and knew we each had psychic ability.

One thing I did not realize right away about my psychic ability, aside from the one isolated tarot card reading, was that I could connect with loved ones who had passed on. It was a couple years later that I realized my natural mediumship ability.

Writing played a critical part in revealing my ability to get messages from the dead. I love to write, and writing helps me heal myself. If I am angry, upset, or just plain confused, I will write and see where the words take me. I am not sure, but sometimes I truly feel they take me to a place either outside of myself, maybe another dimension, or inside of myself, to my inner core. My writing also seems to take on a form of its own, where my thoughts come so quickly. I can't seem to write fast enough and I'm afraid I will forget something since my fingers can't keep up with my gushing mind. Little did I know I would expand my horizons and write about thoughts I was receiving from the departed.

CHAPTER 8
A Father's Connection

A chance encounter with people in my community brought my writing to the forefront.

A group of us from my town gathered at a local function and talk centered on local happenings. A recent misfortune had fallen upon a boy in the community, whose father had passed away some years ago. I had heard of the boy, but didn't know him personally. After hearing the boy's dilemma, I felt sorry for him. I thought to myself, I wish I could help him. Although I am psychic, little did I know what was about to unfold.

I woke up the next morning and decided to write the boy's name, Tom*, on the top of a piece of paper. I closed my eyes and went into a meditative state. I opened my eyes and started writing furiously. Thoughts were flowing through my head, and I wrote them on paper as fast as I could. Sometimes I couldn't keep up, and the words were ahead of what I could write down. A story with messages unfolded from Tom's deceased father, Tim*. Tim was desperate to get in touch with his son. Tim saw his son going down the wrong path and wanted him to change his ways. He knew his son had great potential; actually, God-given talents.

This is an excerpt from my writing:

> *He needs HELP! You (Phyllis) can help him — tell him more about me. I love him with all my heart. Always watching him and getting more & more frustrated that I can't be there to physically help him. You (Phyllis) are a mother; you love to help your children & others. Help my son. Take him off that destructive path he is on. He has to clean up his act. He has to*

believe in you and in turn believe in me. I know how much he loves me and misses me. I'm his hero but I can't fully help him if he doesn't want to help himself. He needs that spark — that ray of hope to guide his nature.

BE THE RAY OF HOPE

Show him; tell him all the wonderful opportunities just waiting for him. He needs to believe in himself and his amazing talents. Take away the cloud that blocks him to see — clear him to see the true world around him. Get out of himself and help others — it will give him confidence — Helping others is so rewarding — He will feel that reward & reap the benefit. Drive away the demons by putting his mind & talent into action. Believe, believe, believe in himself — Have him embrace my love and wear it as a warm blanket, my undying love for him. My child, my beautiful son — who can shine his wondrous light on so many.

There will be masses of people who will greatly benefit from watching him. I am his biggest & best fan. I have a special message sent from above — but always down here with him. Tell him to feel my presence — concentrate — open his mind to my presence and he will feel me. Ask me anything and I will answer him with love always. I smile on him and want to share and care so deeply for him. He is loved immensely — not only by me but his entire family. He has so much support. Revel in that positive energy. Feel its strength and let it lift him to a higher ground. The highest on high he will feel a true high — not artificial — that will know no bounds.

Love is such strength. Prayer — has such positive energy. Many people are praying for him, strength in numbers. This will help him overcome. We shall overcome. He needs to believe in himself. He needs to get professional help and feel the prayers of others. He must pray himself and talk to me. I listen to everything and will show him answers. I love him with all my heart. I am his biggest fan.

(Speaking directly to him) Your mother loves you unconditionally, know this. No matter what you do or say, she never stops loving you & neither do I. You must PLEASE understand this. I LOVE YOU — YOU AS YOU ARE & WHAT YOU WILL BECOME. I see the future for you, and it is GREAT. You are a superstar — let your light shine! Love Dad — Your Dad — one & only.

I was blown away by what I wrote! I actually made a connection with someone I didn't even know, never met, and to top it off, was dead! The power of his words and intentions struck me so deeply. I truly believed that what I wrote was from this boy's deceased father, not my imagination.

Now I had a crucial choice to make. What do I do with this writing? I didn't personally know the boy or his family. Do I muster up the courage and just show up at his doorstep? Do I mail it to him? Do I tell someone who knows his mother to relay the message? There is a woman, we both know, from town. Do I just keep this writing to myself? Decisions, decisions, decisions! It was a tough choice to make, but I knew in my heart and soul which option was the right one to pick.

A couple of weeks passed, and I was out with my son, driving to go shopping for some bathing suits. My son pretty much hates shopping, but skinny dipping was out of the question! At least in my mind. On the ride back home, it hit me. I had to stop at Tom's house and read what I wrote to him. I carried the message with me at all times in case I got the courage. That day was the day; I just knew it.

My son had fallen asleep in the car. He was thirteen at the time, but ever since he was an infant, a car ride could sometimes lull him to sleep. I pulled up to a house, although I wasn't sure if it was the right one. My son woke up and asked what was going on. I told him, and he pleaded with me not to do it. He thought I would look like a crazy woman just showing up at a stranger's house. On top of it, I wanted to read a letter from a dead man! My son was embarrassed. However, I did convince him to tell me which house it was. Against my son's wishes, but definitely honoring Tim's, I got out of the car. My son slouched down in the car seat and stayed there.

I saw three boys on the lawn and walked up to them. I asked who Tom was. One handsome, smiling boy said, "I am." A thought popped into my head to ask him to see his mother, and so I did. Tom replied respectfully, "I'll get her for you." I was amazed at how I was guided and how easy it was all transpiring. No questions asked, this boy happily ran to get his mother.

A beautiful woman stepped out and asked, "Can I help you?" There obviously was no recognition on her face because she had never seen me before and I had never seen her.

Instantly, the words came out of my mouth, "Do you know Sandy*?" Yes, she did. I asked if Sandy spoke about a woman in town who goes Christmas caroling with families at the local group home. She also goes with families to a soup kitchen.

She smiled and said, "Yes, Sandy has. I wanted to volunteer, but have been so busy."

"I'm that woman," I said, "and my name is Phyllis."

Her body seemed to relax. She replied, "What can I help you with?"

Again, words seemed to flow. I said, "This may sound strange, but I have a message from your husband who passed away, and it is for your son, Tom." I showed her my written papers. I held my breath to hear her response.

She stared intently at me for a few seconds and then said, "I'm a believer." Thankfully, I breathed a sigh of relief.

Tom said, "Mom, my friends and I were just leaving to get something to eat." She looked at me, then looked at him and said, "No, Tom, you need to stay and listen to what this woman wrote."

I started to read and within a few seconds started crying, but continued reading. I can't fully describe how emotional it was to be giving this special message to Tom. I continued reading and Tom started to cry. Susan* started crying, too. Tom's older brother, John*, came out from inside the house because he had heard them both crying. Susan explained that I had a message from his dad.

I kept reading, and at one point, I mentioned Tom's yellow sneakers. John asked Tom if he had yellow sneakers; he didn't think he did. Tom replied that they weren't actually yellow but had yellowed with time. He knew the exact sneakers I had written about. Tim gave validation, referring to something his son kept in his room.

I read more and Tom started crying again. When I finished my reading, I didn't know if the words made sense, but I saw the emotional effect on Susan and Tom. Susan thanked me for sharing this message with them. Tom seemed to be dazed by it all, almost in shock. He couldn't speak. John stepped in and thanked me, too.

Susan asked if she could keep the papers, but I said my handwriting is absolutely terrible and she would not be able to read it. I said I would type it up for her and drop it off. She told me that she truly felt that the messages I delivered were from her husband. I was thankful and relieved. I had no idea if what I wrote made sense, but she validated that for me. Both of them, crying, also validated the power of the words that Tim had given me to write.

I felt empowered because I didn't let my fear stop me from relaying Tim's message. I saw the positive emotional affect it had on Tim's wife and son. I knew I was an instrument, working for the greater good.

Tim allowed me to realize I had a gift of connecting with spirits of passed loved ones. I never knew I had that capability. I always watched mediums on TV and saw them in person, but did not expect myself to have those abilities. Tim gave me proof by way of his family's reaction to the words he gave me to write. He was my first connection with spirit through writing. The reason why he chose me . . . I am still unsure. Maybe it is because I am a mother and like to help people. Whatever the reason, I am forever grateful he chose me to relay his messages and gave me the courage to do so. Tim opened my eyes, the two on my face, and also my "third" eye. He gave me sight and insight into my medium abilities.

I got to know his family a little more and realized that Susan and Tom have intuitive abilities. They weren't the only ones. I did a reading for two of the daughters. The first reading was for Alexa*. Afterward, she told me that she had started to realize that she had abilities. We had several discussions about psychic abilities, and I have sent her books in order to expand her knowledge. We keep in touch and help one another out when the occasion arises. Her intuition is truly blossoming. I just know whatever career she chooses, she will put her intuitive abilities to good use by helping people.

The second reading was for Jen*. She was so young when her dad passed that she really didn't know him. She has abilities, too. Here is an excerpt from her reading, which lovingly brought her comfort.

> *My little girl, oh my pretty little girl, how you have grown, but I know since I am always watching you. You do feel my presence at times, I know you do.*
>
> *You are meant to do good in the world. A helper of people and animals. It will come to you soon enough, where your path will lead you.*

CHAPTER 9
Making Connections

Another source of inspiration comes from my spirit guide, Marissa. One day I started writing and, from what I wrote, realized who she was. I am very thankful to her since she helps me receive messages. In my mind's eye, she looks like Pocahontas from the movie, *Night at the Museum.* I'm not sure why and I haven't asked her, but I believe she was a Native American woman in a past life.

I have asked her many questions about various things, both personal and professional. She has answered me quite eloquently every single time. She provided me with a mantra of protection, which I read to myself before every client reading.

> *I am a child of the Lord God. I put white light all over me to protect me. I wear a suit of armor to protect me from any negative/evil entities. They will not encompass me at all. I am shielded, protected by my divine source. God is of love eternal. He has blessed me with a gift for the good of all. I do my work to better mankind (women too!). I serve only him, no one else. I am a healer, a helper of people. I am going to make connections to bless the ones left behind. I will give them guidance and messages from above for good and only good.*
>
> GODSPEED
>
> *We are ready to begin.*
>
> *Love & Blessings,*
>
> *Marissa*

Marissa is my primary spirit guide, but I do have a secondary or occasional spirit guide named Katia. She looks like the good witch from the *Wizard of Oz.* I also rely on my deceased loved ones to help me with my readings or for advice for myself. My mother, father, sister, and grandmother are my primary helpers, and Uncle Tony will help occasionally. Certain Archangels — Michael, Ariel, Rafael, and Metatron — give guidance relating to my intuitive abilities. I am grateful to each of them.

My clients, along with friends and family, have frequently asked me questions, particularly this one. How do you actually connect with a spirit? Although I don't actually know for certain, I can tell you that you probably do it in your everyday life, not connect with spirits, but maybe, daydream.

When you daydream, your mind goes to a different place. Your focus is almost like you are on a different realm. If you look at a person who is daydreaming, their eyes seem to be staring off somewhere else. Some people describe it as if they are staring off into space. Has that happened to you? Think about it. That's what happens to me.

I put my focus on another level, so to speak, like daydreaming. Although the difference is that when I put myself on that level, I guess you could even call it a trance, the spirit connects with me by sending me thoughts. I don't actually hear a voice. The spirit, I surmise, somehow realizes I am ready to receive messages, and they send them to me. I can either start accepting the messages or not.

Once I get the messages, I start typing them. My handwriting is terrible, so to make the messages easier to read, I thought it would be better to type. However, I didn't realize this at first. I had to learn the hard way.

When I first started, I wrote the messages. I could hardly read them myself, much less have someone else read them, like Tim's wife, Susan. So, my next move was to write them and then type from what I had written. I realized quickly enough that it was tedious and time-consuming. I came up with the bright idea of typing the message as soon as I heard it. I wasn't sure if this would work, but VOILA! Typing allowed for the words to appear easily and to be comprehensible. Problem solved!

There is a catch. When I am typing the messages, I go very quickly and sometimes words are missing and/or misspelled. After a reading, I help myself by going back and grammatically correcting what I have written. Once I have done that, I email my client their typed reading. This way, they have a hard copy that they can look back on from time to time and not worry about forgetting the messages. Some clients also record the reading, which is fine. Many clients don't record, so the hard copy is quite beneficial. It is a keepsake for them.

I personally like the idea of having a typed version or recording. When I used to get readings done, I would record them on a tape recorder. Yes, I'm showing my age. I would go back and listen to the recordings maybe six months or a year later to see what came true. I have even gone back many years later and listened again. I save all my recordings and find validation of the reader's ability by re-listening. I truly enjoy doing that.

As I've said previously, it may take many years for a prediction to become a reality. Don't be disappointed if a message doesn't come to fruition right away. It's important to be patient because it may take many years to occur. Remember, the prediction for my mother to reconcile with her family took twenty years to come true!

I must admit, I am not a patient person. I was excited about my newfound gift of connecting with spirits and giving messages. I couldn't wait to try it out even more! About a month after my realization, my husband, two sons, and I were taking a summer vacation to London. I thought it would be great to try my medium abilities on people in London who I didn't know at all!

The vacation was a partial high school graduation present for my son, Sean, and it would be his second meeting with his birth father. Sean is adopted. He is my first miracle. My son, Dean, was a complete shock when I found out I was pregnant five years after adopting Sean. The doctors gave me a one percent chance of ever getting pregnant. Talk about beating the odds!

Sean's birth dad, Aaron, is a wonderful man. He was gracious enough to play "tour guide" for us in London. I can't say enough great things about him. With all his exemplary qualities, he is a true role-model for Sean.

While we were there, Aaron showed us how to use the subway, which was actually quite easy. We spent quite a bit of time getting on and off from our hotel and meeting him at the various sights. "Mind the gap." If you get to London, you will know what it means!

Early on, I got the bright idea of trying out my newfound medium ability while in London. I tested it by looking at a person who was sitting in a subway seat to see if I came up with any visions or messages. Of course, you realize that these people were total strangers, in a different country. I figured if I could come up with something for them, it would prove to me that my gift was real.

I focused on a young woman, probably in her twenties. She looked upset, almost to the point of distraught. I closed my eyes and got a message for her. It was pretty brazen of me, but somehow, I found my inner strength. I walked over to her and said, "I get the feeling you are upset about something, but someone close to you who has passed away wants you to know that it will, in fact, all work out. No need to be upset anymore." She looked at me and started crying. At that point, it was her stop to get off. She ran off the subway and straight to a restaurant. We got off, too. My husband saw her run to the ladies' room. She didn't validate that what I said made sense, but her reaction told me that my feeling was correct. Although, I could have been wrong; she might have run into the ladies' room because she was scared of the "creepy lady!"

Another time I tried it with a man that had put on headphones. I watched him as he seemed to zone out. Suddenly, I had a vision of a large black woman in a caftan and a headdress. She was swaying so easily to music. She gave me a message to tell him not to give up on his music. "He has a job, but that job isn't one where he is pursuing his music. He must get a job that pursues his music. If he does, he will be successful with it."

I tapped him on the shoulder, his eyes opened wide, and I explained the message his grandmother had given me. He thanked me profusely since he had been struggling with which path to take with his music. An enormous smile then appeared on his face. He confirmed the description of his grandmother and said she would give him that advice. His last words to me were, "God bless you." I was amazed that this complete stranger had validated the message that I was given from his departed loved one. I felt more confident about my second reading.

Chapter 10
Missing Boy

Back in the states, I had another opportunity to be contacted by someone. This time, though, it was from a missing boy. A large search was created for a boy, Brandon*. I wondered if Brandon was dead or alive. I didn't know anything about him, but didn't have a good feeling. I wondered if I could think about him and see if I could write anything. Maybe he would contact me. I truly wanted to help people, and if this boy was dead, perhaps I would be able to help with the investigation and thereby bring his family closure. However, I got busy doing other things, and this fell to the wayside.

Dean had a baseball tournament spanning two days that weekend. The first night, we went to dinner, and someone mentioned the missing boy. They still hadn't found him. I thought about him again but got busy again.

Sean came home from college the following weekend. On Sunday, my family and I went to a pancake place. As I stood, standing by the door, I saw a poster with the missing boy's picture. I thought it strange to be at that restaurant, which was about forty-five minutes away. It got me thinking about him again. About three nights later, I woke up around 3 AM and couldn't sleep. This happens quite a bit. I either read or listen to a meditation to put me back to sleep.

I went to the spare room to lie down. In a relaxed state, I thought about Brandon and started writing. He had been missing for two weeks. Thus far, I have only connected with people who have passed away, not the living. Sadly, Brandon connected with me immediately. I just knew he was dead.

He gave descriptions of where he died. He had strong messages for his mother and for young men like himself. He felt he had made wrong choices, and that's how he ended up like he did. I felt he was a good soul who wanted his message given to others so they would not end up like him, a life filled with promise, but short-lived. He wanted to help others.

I was now left with a dilemma. What should I do with this writing, this message from the missing boy? It reminded me of when I got the messages from Tim for his son and wasn't sure what to do. However, this was quite different. I looked on the internet to see if Brandon had been found, but after two weeks, he still hadn't been located. It appeared that no one knew he was dead.

I wrestled with who I should contact about my writing. My choices were the police or Brandon's mother. I shuffled my tarot cards and thought about his mother. Two cards came up — the queen card — which I believe represented his mother. The other card was a young man. Behind him was a second face with lines drawn in front of it. This card, I believe, represented the boy who showed one side of his face to his mother, but the other side was hidden from her. Consequently, I felt at this point that going to see his mother wasn't the answer.

I decided to go to the police, with the message I had written. I was a little apprehensive at first; I had never done this before. I had some worries about the police believing a *medium*. They might wonder if I could give accurate information. I would have to say that I received a message from the boy who passed. I might encounter non-believers. The police may listen to what I had to say, then laugh the second I left and throw the message right into the garbage. Although I knew in my heart, I had to go to the police.

A sense of peace followed by confidence came over me. I asked Brandon to help me stay strong in order to deliver the message. While I was driving to the police station, the song *Believer* rang out on the radio. I felt it was a sign and thought the person I was going to speak with could be a believer.

With paper in hand, I walked up to the police station. I wasn't nervous, well, maybe just a tad. I went up to the window and said I had some information about the missing boy. The man said to take a seat. He came back in about five minutes and told me the detective would be out shortly. I waited for about ten minutes.

The detective was cordial and brought me into a tiny room. I said I had some information, but it was going to sound a bit strange. At that point, my nerves started to act up. Again, I said it would sound strange. I told the detective that I read about the missing boy. I mentioned instances where he was brought up at dinner and again at the pancake house. I said the boy was on my mind and that morning, at 3 AM, I had woken up and started writing.

He immediately put me at ease and said the police deal with mediums and psychics on a regular basis. A medium had already been to see him. I felt much better hearing that, so I asked if I could read him what I wrote. I started reading, and he patiently listened to me. At one point, I almost started crying but stopped myself. I didn't want to break down. I continued reading, then finished. He asked me some questions. I thought the answers were pretty apparent in the reading, but I answered, re-reading some parts for clarification. He said the police were taking each and every lead and treating them fairly. He said he had been in touch with the family the day before.

The detective thanked me for the information and gave me his card. If anything else came to me, he would like to know. The boy was still missing after two weeks. He said, hopefully some good news would come about him still being alive. I looked at him in disbelief, having just said that this boy told me he was dead. I wasn't sure where this detective was coming from. He then looked at me and said that in his years of experience with the police force, he believed it was not likely he was alive. He thanked me again, shook my hand, and said goodbye.

I felt a sense of relief that I had shared this information. I wanted to honor this boy and help him by sharing the information he had given me. In my heart, it felt truly great and rewarding. I wasn't focused on how crazy or "out there" I might appear. My focus was on him.

A few weeks later, it was announced Brandon was found dead. If I aided in putting a few pieces of the puzzle together, I am satisfied. If I didn't, at least I tried. My prayers and condolences go out to his family. They had raised a wonderful boy who had good values. He went down the wrong path with his choices. In the end, he shared messages from beyond for the betterment of mankind, a truly selfless act indeed.

When Brandon put the idea in my mind to go to his wake, I didn't hesitate. Now, this may take you by surprise. I didn't know Brandon in the physical world, but I definitely got to know him through the spiritual world. I loved his essence, his soul. I wanted to honor him when he asked.

Brandon has since given me songs that I just *know* are from him. He has sent me signs. I have a total of ten readings from him. Most of them are for his mother. At this point in time, I have not given them to her. Brandon still lets me know that it is not the right time. When he feels it is, you can bet I will gladly find her, come hell or high water, and deliver them.

I made sure to connect with Brandon. I will make sure I connect, in an earthly way, with Brandon's mom. When I do, I suspect that I will see Brandon in her eyes. I believe the writings from him will give her some peace, comfort, and joy. I just *know* she is deserving of this, like her son.

CHAPTER 11

Random Connections

I have had only a few occasions when a passed loved one would try to get my attention, even though I was not trying to connect. However, they were definitely trying to connect with me, to give a message to their loved one.

One instance comes to mind: it was when I was getting my hair dyed. I was waiting in the chair, with color all over my head. My grey hairs had been coming in more quickly. As I sat there, I kept hearing a message: "Ask the woman next to you why she came so early to get her hair dyed. She typically waits six weeks before getting it dyed." The thought kept coming to me and I was thinking, *I'm not going to say a word to that woman.*

You see, it was my first time at this hair salon, and I didn't want people to think I was a nut job! However, the deceased woman was extremely persistent. I gave in and asked the woman next to me if she had come in earlier than usual to get her hair dyed. "Yes," she replied, "as a matter of fact, I did come only three weeks from the last time. I typically come every six weeks, but I am going to Florida for a family reunion. I wanted my hair to look nice and didn't want to wait."

She looked at me a little puzzled and wanted to know why I asked. I asked her if she had a grandmother who passed away. She said she did and in fact was quite close to her. She missed her all the time. I told her this may sound strange, but I can connect with people who have passed away. I described her grandmother since I could see her in my mind's eye.

I do not mean to stereotype old Italian women, but in my mind, I saw that her grandmother wore all black, was short and plump. She was stirring a big pot of "gravy" — tomato sauce, as you may call it. The woman started crying and validated that it was her. Every Sunday, it was a tradition for her to make the gravy, and the family would come over and eat together.

The woman confided in me that she was torn about believing in spirits connecting with mediums. She said she was a devout Christian, and the church didn't believe in such things. She really wanted to believe, but felt guilty because of her faith.

Her grandmother was quite a character! I will quote exactly what she said to tell her granddaughter: "*Va fungool* the church! I am the one speaking to you, so you better believe!"

I almost fell off my chair, and the woman burst into belly laughter! She said, "Well, that definitely is my grandmother!"

I can't make this stuff up! This is sincerely a true incident that I had at the hair salon.

Another time, I was at the dentist's office, waiting for my x-rays to be taken. A young woman walked in and said, "Please bear with me. I wasn't scheduled to take your x-rays today, but the other girl is busy." I got a message, "Ask her about tarot cards." I also had a vision of a woman standing at a sink wearing a housecoat, with curlers in her hair and a cigarette hanging out of her mouth.

I followed through and asked the young woman if she had a grandmother who passed away that she was close to. The young woman answered yes, so I described exactly what I saw. She confirmed it was her grandmother! I told her that her grandmother said to ask her about the tarot cards. The woman told me her grandmother used to read tarot cards. The week before, the young woman went into a holistic store and felt the urge to buy a deck of tarot cards.

I said that her grandmother wanted her to start practicing because she has a gift for reading them, just like her grandmother did. The young woman was amazed by this message, especially since she was thinking of taking a class on how to read them. Her grandmother definitely approved!

CHAPTER 12

Returning the Favor

My most powerful communicator is Tim. Remember, he is the deceased father of the boy, Tom, whom I helped. Periodically, he lets me know when it is time to give his family members messages. I have since given more messages to Tom, Susan, Alexa, and Jen. They hold a special place in my heart. I am thankful they were gracious and open-minded enough to accept me, a stranger to them. Their kindness and compassion allowed me to speak Tim's words. We all cried together. Tim and Susan raised their children with a strong faith. We rejoiced together, knowing spirit lives on. We reveled knowing spirit continues to love and help us. Tim wanted his son to flourish and share his talents for people to appreciate. What a blessing!

I helped Tim in his son's time of need, and Tim returned the favor for me. I want to share a private feeling with you. I started doing medium readings at a holistic center in 2017. The key word is started. The first time I did, I had four clients. The second time, only two. I also taught classes there for tarot card reading. More people turned out for classes than for medium readings. I was scheduled to do four readings in the month. The following month, the owner said she wouldn't put medium readings on her calendar for clients.

I guessed that, logically, not much money was coming in with the medium readings, so she decided to skip a month or two to build up interest and get more people scheduled. However, I'm not always logical. Fear and doubt sometimes dance around in my head. I started to think that perhaps she thought I wasn't such a great medium, and that's why not many people were coming. You know when you assume . . . I started doubting my abilities. I had proof from previous experiences, but they seemed to wash away, disappear down the drain. Self-doubt can be cruel.

For some reason, I was going through old paperwork. I happened to find something I wrote. I had forgotten all about it. It was from Tim, the deceased father of the boy I helped. His words for me were as follows:

> BE THE CHANGE PHYLLIS—*do kind acts—use your God-given gift to help others. Make other people happy and give them hope for a life beyond. Tell them their future — connect with their loved ones. They are waiting to hear from you. I will help you bring them their loved one's messages and stories. Connect — it's what you do best. Speak to them — Speak publicly. Now you know how and are comfortable. Be their ray of hope and compassion. You have it inside you, let it out for all the world to benefit and appreciate. No, it's not you thinking, it's me talking! I made you look at that article. (One was written about him describing his good qualities.) We have similar attributes. Use your gift like you told my son Tom to use his. I am telling you like you told Tom. I see what goes on and like Tom, you are meant to do good things in the world.*
>
> BE THE CHANGE
>
> *Think about this Phyllis and then:*
> JUST DO IT — *like you tell your students and clients.*
> *I will help you.*
>
> *Love (in a friendly way) Tim*

I couldn't believe what I read! Tim had given me those words of encouragement. I really needed to hear them again because I doubted my abilities. He gave me HOPE. He gave me COURAGE. He gave me INSPIRATION!

I went to read four women, and before I started, I heard Pharrell Williams' song, *Happy*, playing in my head. I felt it was a good sign. To my delight, the readings went extremely well. I connected easily with my client's loved ones. Messages were so strong and crucial for them to hear. There was crying, healing, and hope for all of them. Each woman gave me a heartfelt hug. They embraced me and, in effect, gave me reassurance of my abilities.

Those readings were the most powerful at the holistic center. All the women who I read did something I did not expect. They sang my praises to the owner. One woman was so impressed that she said she was going to write her comments on the owner's website. A stellar review would be mine. She also gave me a generous tip. That had never happened before. It wasn't the money that made me feel good. It was the act of wanting to give me something extra for that which she felt I had given to her.

These women validated my abilities. Doubt was slain, fear evaporated, and exuberance filled me. The joy I felt must have shined through because one woman said I was glowing. A soulful lesson was learned that day, thanks to the help from Tim. The words he gave me came true. He helped me connect so easily with their loved ones. His inspiration fueled me to be unafraid to share my God-given talents with women who needed them so very much. I shared hope, courage, and inspiration with them. I will be forever grateful to his ethereal spirit.

Pause here for a moment. Think about Tim's words for yourself whenever you have self-doubt. We all go through it. Let Tim's words raise you up to fiercely believe in yourself!

Tim called on me another time while I was on the treadmill. He wanted me to help his son again. I was watching one of Oprah's *Super Soul Sundays*, an old one. She had a man on, Devon Franklin, who wrote the book, *Produced by Faith*. He, too, had lost his father when he was about eight years old. He became successful and always put his faith first, above all else.

I just *knew* Tim wanted his son to read the book. He wanted the book to inspire his son to trust in his faith to guide him to success. My son ordered the book for me. It was delivered rather quickly, but for some reason, I held on to it. Then the right time presented itself. That day was Valentine's Day. Yes, Tim wanted it delivered on the day when love is most honored and revered. I also knew I had to do a reading for Tom and Susan. I did one for each. I texted Susan and said I'd be coming over, and if she was not home, I would just leave the book and writings.

Susan was home and happy to see me. We talked a little bit about what I wrote, but she said she would read it later. I said she could mail the book and letter to her son at college. She could tell him the book was from her if she felt more comfortable with that, or say it was from me. The writing would be from me.

To my surprise, she said her son had left the college he originally started. It hadn't worked out there. He was home and going to a college close by. I really didn't know what to say. I had no idea. Remember, I don't know everything. The writing didn't mention this.

While we were talking, something caught my eye out the window. I said to her, "Who is outside playing basketball?" She said it must be Tom. She looked out and, sure enough, it was Tom with a friend. She said, "I thought they were going out."

At that point, I just knew his dad had him stay home so he could see and talk to me. I was so excited Tom was home! I had no expectation of seeing him because I assumed he was away at college. I was elated because all I could think about was giving him a heartfelt hug and having Tom feel all the love his father had for him.

My smile was beaming when I greeted Tom. I hugged him so tight and repeated to him, "You are such a good boy." I felt like I didn't want to let him go. It felt like I could have stayed a lifetime hugging him and having him feel the love. The love was like a cure-all for him. I knew Tim was sending his loving energy through me. Reluctantly, I let go, and we sat down.

I told him about the book his father wanted him to read. I also gave Tom the writing from his father. He said he would read it later. Tom seemed more distant this time when I saw him, but I wasn't sure why. I asked him if I could see one of his games, now that he would be playing for a college close by. We talked a little more, and then he left.

Susan said she wanted to meet me for lunch and explain more of what was going on. I said I'd be happy to. She was going to read the writing I gave her later, in private. She knew she would cry and wanted to be alone with her feelings.

The next day she texted me:

> *Thank you so much for that wonderful gift you shared with my son and me on the most perfect day! The things you wrote were right on and were a confirmation it was truly my husband speaking to you!!! Let's try to plan a lunch next week and I'll tell you why! God bless!!! Xoxo*

Chapter 13
Dreams

The morning I was going to meet Susan for lunch, I fell back to sleep and had a dream. My son, Dean, was driving a golf cart, and I was sitting next to him. We were driving to Susan's house. Dean was going to pick up Susan's youngest son, who was around Dean's age. Dean wanted to hang out with him at our house.

We got to the house and saw Tom. He was smiling and happy to see us. His youngest sister, Jen, also saw us and was smiling. She said she would get her mother, thinking I was there to do a reading for her mom and brother.

There was a party going on; it was July, but it seemed like a Christmas in July theme. I looked around and saw all the food, decorations, and a bunch of people. I knew Susan was responsible for doing it all. When Jen asked her mom if she would come over and talk to me, she told her no. She just didn't have any time today because she was too busy with the party.

Before Jen could come back and tell me, a young boy came up to me and introduced himself. He didn't look familiar, and I wasn't sure who he was. I got a sense he was quite wise and knowledgeable for his age, like an old soul.

Jen told me her mom wasn't available today. I said I wasn't there to do medium readings, but Dean and I wanted to pick up her younger brother. That was the end of the dream. I knew there was no younger brother. Tom was the youngest boy of the family and Jen was the youngest child.

That was the dream I told Susan about at lunch. I had a feeling I knew what it meant, and she validated it for me. She said she had two miscarriages after her youngest child. She felt her husband was letting her know; one of her miscarriages was a boy. That boy would have been Dean's age. I feel the boy in the dream is with his father and is a loving soul. It's amazing what dreams can reveal and how they can be used for clarification.

Dreams can also give very powerful messages. I firmly believe in writing down dreams as soon as you can. If you do this, you don't run the risk of forgetting. I'm glad I followed my own advice. The following is the dream that saved my life.

I dreamt that I was in my parents' house. I was in my old bedroom when the phone rang at 5 AM. (During the 1970s we had a princess phone with push buttons. It sat on a little table that was in front of the third small bedroom.) Dean walked into my bedroom and said to me, "Mom, maybe it's school calling because we don't have school today." I had a feeling it wasn't school, but instead something bad. Typically, you don't get a phone call that early in the morning. I answered the phone, only to hear my father's voice. (My father had been dead for twenty-two years, but I knew his voice instantly.) He said, "Please take me to the hospital now." I said, "But Dad, can't you wait until later today? We have an appointment later." He said, "No! We have to go now!" That was my dream.

I called my brother that day to tell him about the dream with our dad. We like to call each other and share our dreams about our loved ones that have passed. Sometimes we try to figure out what they mean, but it really isn't easy. I told him, "Daddy is telling me someone will be going to the hospital. I have no idea who that will be, but I just *know* Daddy is representing someone who will have to go to the hospital." We were both puzzled as to who this would be.

A couple of days after my dream, I started to get really chapped lips. They were so dry, peeling and cracked that I was desperate to find a cure. I tried different lip balms, but nothing seemed to really help. This went on for a couple of days, and each day, they looked worse. I looked online to see if I could find a remedy.

I found one that looked like it could work. It said to mix one tablespoon of honey with three teaspoons of sugar as a paste and apply to the cracked lips. I tried it about four times that day. My lips got a little smoother but seemed to swell. Eventually, my lips looked like I just had a full Botox injection. I compared them to the movie *First Wives Club* with Goldie Hawn, where she gets the injections, and her lips are about three times the size.

I have small lips to begin with, so for them to get bigger might not seem outrageous for a normal person, but to me, they looked enormous! That night I told my husband I wasn't feeling right. I started getting dizzy and nauseous. My lips really hurt too, and they seemed to be throbbing and expanding at the same time. I figured the chapping was getting worse. I went to bed around 9:30 PM, my usual time. (I am an early riser and definitely a morning person.)

I woke up a little after midnight. I told my sleeping husband, "I have to go to the emergency room."

He looked at me through his sleepy eyes. "What are you talking about?" he asked. I just KNEW that was what I had to do. I didn't feel dizzy anymore, but still felt nauseous. I felt strong enough to drive myself and told him to stay in bed. I knew he had an early morning meeting so there was no need to go with me. I also wanted him home for my son, who had to get up early in the morning to go to school.

I was on a mission, even though I didn't know the details, because I was being guided to go to the hospital. Upon arrival, I told the intake nurse that my lips were really swollen, I was sick to my stomach, and I needed to see a doctor. At this point, I still didn't understand what was wrong with me. The doctor took one look at me and said I was having an allergic reaction. He wanted to know how my throat was and I said it was pretty scratchy.

He asked if I had eaten something out of the ordinary. I said the only thing I could think of was honey, but I didn't eat it. I put it on my lips as a remedy for my chapped lips. Come to think of it, I told him, I used a honey lip balm, too. He believed that was the culprit and informed me that I would immediately need to be put on an IV. A nurse came in with IV bags of prednisone, Benadryl, and Pepcid. I was shocked, but another part of me knew this was the solution.

When the nurse left, I felt a calm come over me. I wasn't alone. I could feel my deceased father, mother, and sister there were with me, which brought me comfort. I want to thank the second nurse who checked on me about an hour or so after the first nurse left. She comforted me by lowering the bed so I could be in a sleeping position instead of sitting upright. She also put a blanket on top of me to help keep me warm and gave me the call bell, in case I needed her for anything.

The compassion I felt from her was undeniable and unexplainable. She seemed like an angel to me and, who knows, maybe she actually was. I didn't see her again before I left. Before being discharged, I saw the first nurse again who didn't possess the same caring qualities. I'm sending my angelic second nurse a heartfelt thank you, whether she is, in fact, real or surreal.

Speaking of surreal, a thought popped into my head about the meaning of my dream with my father. To my unbelievable surprise, I was the one who went to the hospital! I didn't wait until later that day. I felt my father wake me in the middle of the night so I could go to the hospital and be cured. If that didn't happen, perhaps I could have suffocated in my sleep and died. Like the doctor said, I was having an allergic reaction. The doctor prescribed prednisone and Benadryl to take at home, along with a prescription for an epi-pen. The strange thing is, I never liked honey and never had it. I had no clue that I was allergic to it. You may want to take this incident to heart yourself and get checked for allergies. I know I am going to get checked for any other allergies I may have, but am not aware of.

I thank my father for saving my life by giving me my dream and waking me up to go to the hospital. I must have more purpose left on this earth. I have an uncanny feeling it is related to helping people.

I had another very memorable dream, and this time, it was from my grandmother, Carmella, who tried to help me. Remember, I was only four years old when she passed away. I never had a dream about her until the ripe old age of forty-seven. That dream was definitely worth waiting for. First, a little background.

Similar to my grandmother, my mother liked money. They both liked earning it. Saving it was also a high priority for them. Their differences appeared in how they invested it. My grandmother liked investing in real estate. Remember, she owned a house and two rental properties. My mother, however, liked to invest in stocks.

We had neighbors up the street from us who liked to dabble in the stock market. The husband was a math teacher and his bride, a housewife. They both spent time learning about the market and investing. Their investments paid off quite well. My mother was friendly with the wife, and they started talking about stocks. Since money could be made, and my mom liked to learn about things that interested her, she received some lessons from the couple. My mom became truly fascinated and ended up doing well with it. My father had no desire to learn, but trusted my mother with his paycheck, which he handed over to her every week. At that time, it was unusual for a man to have his wife handle the household money. I guess my mother was a pioneer when it came to money. She and my grandmother had that in common. I handle the household money, too, although my husband is very capable. Today, it's not as uncommon as it was years ago for women to do so. Thankfully!

My mom passed along her knowledge of money to me at an early age and I was hooked. Maybe that's why I like to give presentations on financial literacy. Unlike my mom, who taught her three children, I like to pass along my knowledge to a larger crowd. Our childhoods do play a part in our future.

My mother bought me stocks when I was quite young. I started buying stocks from the time I started earning a paycheck. The market did well for me, and I continued to invest. My attitude toward investing was "slow and steady wins the race." For quite a while, I was lucky to have no major upsets, only small ones along the way.

So, here we go! In the dream, my grandmother said to sell all my stocks and put the money in the bank. She didn't give an explanation.

First, I couldn't believe I dreamt about my grandmother. After forty-three years, she decided to come to me in a dream. Second, I thought she was crazy! Who in their right mind would do such a thing? I rationalized it away. I figured that since she had never invested in stocks during her life, she didn't know what she was talking about.

I overlooked one thing . . . an important one at that. She made her living predicting the future. For whatever reason, that fact eluded me at the time. I stubbornly stuck to my assumption of her ignorance and didn't listen to the message she gave me in the dream. My smugness cost me in more ways than one.

Sadly, a few days after my dream, we experienced the 2008 stock market crash. Some of you may have also experienced it and may still be cringing! Some of you may have been lucky and only heard about it. Alas, much of my investment went down the proverbial drain.

Well, you know what they say when you assume. I sure made an ass of myself and lost quite a bit of money. If I had listened to my grandmother's advice, I would be a richer woman today! I did get back into the market again, but proceeded with more caution. If my grandmother ever comes to me again in a dream, I will follow her exact advice without hesitation. Hopefully, she will give me another chance!

My grandmother tried to help me. Her prediction came true. Shame on me for not believing her! I think my ego got the best of me. In more ways than one, it was a very valuable lesson learned. I know it is harder for me to accept help because I prefer giving help.

CHAPTER 14
Talker

Throughout my life, I have always enjoyed helping people. You may do the same thing. There are plenty of people who purposely volunteer or do random acts of kindness. I love to think that's what makes the world go round.

In some way, each job I had allowed me the opportunity to help clients, students, co-workers, and bosses. I have volunteered for several non-profits, which I see as a win-win situation. I help someone in some way, and in turn, I am also getting satisfaction and gratification.

I'm a communicator, a *talker*, so when I talk to people, I feel I am helping them. I'll strike up a conversation with total strangers and truly enjoy hearing their stories. I don't have a problem talking to people in the grocery store, car wash, beauty salon, or even on vacation. Just ask my kids. My son, Dean, is especially embarrassed about this trait I have. My son, Sean, just gives me a look and walks away when he's with me. Dean gives me a lecture on how *creepy* I am. I can't figure him out. He doesn't have a problem with me talking to complete strangers who are dead, but with living strangers, it's an issue for him.

I admit, sometimes I will go on and on if the person I'm talking to allows it. Actually though, I think I am more of a conversationalist. As much as I like to talk, I also enjoy listening to what the other person has to say. A conversation that is two-sided is more up my alley, so to speak.

Moving along those lines, I guess it makes some sense that the dead "talk" to me. Although, let me rephrase that more appropriately: "send me messages." Remember, I don't hear their actual voices, and I don't have to worry if I can understand their language. They send me thoughts. I have asked them questions at times, so we do have a conversation. The dead are very willing to communicate with me since not many amongst the living can communicate with them. However, I can't say the same about the living. They all can communicate, but don't always want to carry on a *conversation* with me, the talker!

I know one particular person who is notorious for being a *talker.* Seriously, this person kept someone on the phone for five, yes you read that right, five hours! When this person is spotted at a party, most people make a mad dash! You may know a person like that, or you may be that person!

Chapter 15
Hiding the Truth

For a talker like me, you would think I had no problem talking about my abilities. However, fear can often win over logic. At first, I didn't feel confident telling people I had this ability. When I told people that I was an accountant and CPA, they looked at me as if I had truly accomplished something. When I was an adjunct professor, people admired my dedication. There was a sense of respect, level-headedness, and credibility with both professions.

This is not the case with being a psychic or medium. There still seems to be a stigma around it because some people are quite skeptical. Others go to the extreme and believe that people who call themselves psychics or mediums are just downright crazy! I've heard people use the phrases, "off their rocker," "looney toons," "freaks" and "not playing with a full deck." Do they mean playing cards or tarot cards?

Some people believe this profession is composed of all scam artists. They think we just make up stuff and laugh as the "sucker" walks away. You can understand, then, why I was scared to expose myself.

Taking a leap of faith and not caring about what other people thought of me was difficult, if not terrifying! I'm a more reserved person, unlike my sister who didn't give a "rat's ass" (her expression, not mine) what people thought of her. She would say, "They could go scratch!" The "f" word was also present in her vocabulary, but not mine. Remember, my sister was kind of like the black sheep of the family and oh, how I loved her for it!

I had my husband's love and support. He took more of my sister's approach. He told me to focus on myself and what makes me happy. Mitch believed my newfound gift right from the start. Some people close to me are still skeptical, and that is just fine. We each have to form our own beliefs. Mitch encouraged me to pursue my new career and said I should write a book about it. Well, I'm glad I finally acted upon his advice. I hope you are, too!

Mitch even created a space for me to do my readings and give classes. He is a Mr. Fixit at heart, even though accounting is his trade. Yes, we are both CPA's, go figure! It was his love and support that made it easier and allowed me to flourish. He said not to waste time worrying about what other people thought. I am forever grateful to him.

My son, Sean, completely agreed. He helped me create flyers and email databases for psychic events. When in doubt about technology, go to your child. Sean was and still is a wealth of knowledge and support in both areas. I am truly grateful to him.

Unfortunately, I wasn't as confident as Pat, Mitch, and Sean. I tried to keep my psychic abilities and pursuits quiet, at least for a while. I didn't want my tax clients, colleagues, or students to know. I figured if they did, I would be a laughingstock and lose business as well. I worried about my son, Dean, who was thirteen at the time. You know kids can be cruel, and I didn't want him to experience any backlash. I asked him what he thought of my letting parents of his classmates know I could do medium and psychic readings. Dean simply replied, "Mom, it's fine. You do you!" I was so surprised. What a relief! I realized I worried for nothing. Kids can be less complicated or "hung-up" than adults about certain things.

Into the water I dove! Not! I hesitantly put in my little toe. I did readings that were a distance from my house. I also taught classes that were further away. I figured the odds of me running into someone I knew were lower than if I worked somewhere close to my home. The law of statistics was on my side. For a time, it worked.

However, questions kept swirling. Did I want to show the world I was someone different from the persona they knew? Was I brave enough not to care what people thought of me? Should I take the risk and have people think less of me? Could I handle people making fun of me, to my face or behind my back? I had a place in society where I didn't stand out. I realized I had a gift that could make me stand out as being different, possibly in a negative way.

I found direction by asking my spirit guide, Marissa, and my grandmother, Carmella. They gave me messages not to worry about any negative reactions. I took their advice and went within myself. I finally listened to the same intuition I had offered to others. The words were, "Be yourself and accept your truth. Fear does not come from God. God gave you this gift to share with others. There is no reason to doubt or be ashamed. Rejoice in knowing." This is my philosophy. It may not be yours, but that's fine. I am not looking to persuade or demand. I hope you can ponder.

We all have special gifts. People don't always commend others for their special gifts or for just being themselves. I feel we need to be more conscious of reveling in other people's talents, successes, and the essence of them just being themselves. We may look, act, believe, or think differently, but we should all have compassion and acceptance for one another. No need to hide the differences. Unfortunately, there still remains a stigma around "different" — not the norm. Who decides the norm? I guess we can blame society. Who makes up society? It is each one of us.

What would happen if each and every one of us made a conscious effort to accept? It doesn't mean we should necessarily agree, but allow the other person to just be. Life would be so much easier if that were the case, but sadly it is not now. I pray we will all experience that one fine day. In the meantime, find your inner courage to "just be you" or as Dean puts it, "you do you."

If you are in a similar predicament, please re-read the words my intuition gave me and use them for yourself! Whatever you may be hiding, I wish strength for you. I pray confidence and courage become infused in you.

Think about this. Who was I really hiding from? Myself! Ask yourself if you are doing the same. My advice is to accept yourself first. I know first-hand that this can be quite difficult. To quote Suze Orman (I just love her, especially during my financial literacy days, and continue to do so), even though she relates this to money, it can be related to "coming out." "STAND IN YOUR TRUTH." Take a few moments to truly reflect on that phrase.

When you are at peace with who you are, that peace will radiate to others. They will be affected by it, and you, in turn, will be able to handle whatever comes your way. My spirit guide, Marissa, gave me the following messages:

THE CONGRUITY BUILDS LINKS,
NOT CHINKS IN YOUR CHAIN.

IN THE LIGHT, TRUTH SHINES THROUGH —
FIND YOUR TRUTH IN THE LIGHT.

DO WHAT BRINGS YOU JOY
FOR JOY BRINGS SOLACE.

Thank you, dear Marissa, for sharing your wisdom with me. I am happy to share these thought-provoking words. This is another pause for reflection.

I believe we are on a path. Hopefully, the experiences we encounter teach us lessons we need to learn. These lessons that we "keep in our pocket," are lessons we may need to use down the road. The path becomes more difficult when we need to learn new lessons or relearn the old ones we missed because we didn't "reach into our pocket." If we choose to do so, the path may be easier for a time.

CHAPTER 16
Late Bloomer

I do question timing. Why did I realize I could read tarot cards and then connect with the dead later in life? Is it because I had more time to focus on it? That could be the case since my children were in their teens and more self-sufficient. Also, I was denied funding for my financial literacy program at the community college and was out of that job. Could those be the reasons? Could it be because I had developed more skills by running a business and presenting to people? Could it be, deep down, I was finally ready to accept this dormant aspect of myself?

I asked my spirit guide, Marissa, and this was the message she gave:

> *You had to go through many, many lessons to get to the point where you could open yourself up more. You also needed to become more spiritual. You needed to be less self-centered and focus on others more, which you can clearly see now. It was a gradual process to ease you in.*
>
> *If it all happened at once, you would have completely denied it. Think about this and you will realize it is true. You, the student, needed to be ready. Your experiences had to have happened.*
>
> *Your trust needed to open more. Your belief in yourself had to be more open. For these reasons, that is why it took a long time for you to realize your abilities. They were always there.*

Wow! When I read those words, they definitely made sense. I was on the right track when I answered the questions I had asked myself. On a deeper level, though, this reasoning could apply to many people. Although late bloomers are all over the place, "late bloomer" can also be used to describe a certain aspect, or aspects, of a person's life. In other aspects, they are right on time or ahead of the game.

I am a late bloomer in certain aspects of my life. I married Mitch when I was twenty-nine and he was twenty-seven. That could classify me as a late bloomer. We both happened to work in the accounting field. Most married people don't work in the same field. People assumed we met in college getting our accounting degrees or that we worked together. These would be logical assumptions. However, we met at what I refer to as a "dance club." Ask Mitch, and he'll say we met in a bar. Like a typical married couple, we do see things differently at times. I think I said that politely. We are still married after thirty years. Tactfulness sure comes in handy!

Mitch and I adopted our son when we were in our later thirties. We tried various fertility treatments, but were unsuccessful. The doctor gave me a one percent chance of ever getting pregnant. However, we were very successful with adoption. We contacted an adoption lawyer in April, and were holding our two-day-old son, Sean, in November. That was shorter than the time for being pregnant. I feel Sean was miracle one.

I am a late bloomer with getting pregnant with Dean, miracle two. I sure beat the odds with him — ninety-nine to one! At the ripe old age of forty-two, I was pregnant. About a month before I realized I was pregnant, my cousin, Theresa, had a dream. In the dream, her deceased mother told her about my baby coming. Theresa told me about the dream, and both of us were shocked and in disbelief. We both knew my long history of infertility. Yet, Theresa's intuitive abilities through dreams rang true once again.

Take a moment now and think of an area in your life where you could be considered a late bloomer. Re-read the answer from my spirit guide and see if it makes sense for you. Maybe it can apply to you or someone you know. Either way, lessons are learned sooner or later.

Chapter 17
First Fundraiser

One of the main lessons I learned in life is to help others. I'm not a late bloomer in that aspect of my life . . . it has been a common theme throughout. The psychic fundraiser was another opportunity. We were raising money for a non-profit organization so that they, in turn, could help others learn about the amazing history of Baird House.

Sometimes in life, the path can be easier "with a little help from my friends" (to quote a Beatles song). I am truly blessed by my friend Pam. She introduced me to Pat, the president of a nonprofit that runs a historic landmark, Baird House, in our town. Between the three of us, we came up with the idea of a "psychic" fundraiser. Pam and I agreed to organize the event. We had to contact psychics, create a flyer, come up with revenue estimates, and give a presentation to their board of directors.

When something is meant to be, the universe allows things to flow easily. The psychics I knew were available and eager to participate. Pam helped me with the flyer. We were guided to the perfect picture to use, along with descriptions and layout. Being an accountant, I found it easy to develop spreadsheets of the estimated revenues. Having been an adjunct professor and presenter on financial literacy, speaking in front of people came easily to me. My prior experiences prepared me to be confident when explaining the benefits of a psychic fundraiser to the board.

Even though I had transitioned from being an accountant, professor, and speaker, I used the skills associated with them in my psychic/medium profession. In essence, I didn't abandon who I was. I added to my abilities and put them in a new realm. I didn't have a new persona, but an enhanced one. I love analogies . . . it's like I went for a complete makeover — hair, makeup, clothes, and shoes. I looked different, but it was still me. My essence and prior history were the same. What had changed was the way people viewed me and how I looked at myself.

I would be exposed to people in my town at the psychic fundraiser. Wow! It was a scary yet exhilarating thought. It was a combination of a new me and old me on display. I was eager to accept my combination, but would other people? How could I handle this? I thought about what my intuition told me and made it my mantra. It was my battle cry!

At our presentation to the board, I continued to "get a little help from my friends." There were actually several that helped. Denise Graziano, an excellent medium and speaker, gave impressive descriptions of the psychic services we would each provide. Kathy Pascucci, Denise's business partner, who is also an excellent medium, spoke about how the two of them would work as a team doing readings. These two women offer a variety of services in their business, although séances are one of their specialties. This fundraiser couldn't accommodate séances, but their unique way of doing readings is quite appealing and intriguing.

Sal Cavallo, my brother-in-law, spoke robustly about the need to generate more awareness of the historic house and its connection to spirit. Sal would be doing tarot card readings at the fundraiser. He has excellent intuitive abilities. Sal truly enjoys interacting with clients while giving his readings and I have seen his clients reciprocate. We all played our part as a team, and we won! The board approved our proposal!

However, now we needed more help setting up the psychic fundraiser. We enlisted Jeff Carpenter, an actual rocket scientist, who had transformed into a medium, medical intuitive, and Reiki Master. Jeff would be providing Reiki for the fundraiser. He gallantly came to our rescue.

Jeff created a section on his website that was dedicated to giving information about our psychic fundraiser. Among Jeff's long list of talents, he is an excellent writer. He made it easy for a potential client to click on each reader's name and their bio would be revealed. To guarantee a time slot, another click would allow a potential client to choose and book their reading. I am technologically challenged, so his feat was especially impressive.

Carol Wingerter, also an excellent Reiki master, was part of our fundraiser, too. She does Reiki and various kinds of healing. Carol has worked on me several times and she is awesome with her craft! To help our cause, she connected with our town's online newspaper to get an article written about the event. She, too, gave us great advice during our various meetings.

Filomena DeBronzo rounded out our group of seven. She is a seasoned medium, psychic, and reverend who is very gifted and quite spiritual. She also teaches classes. Her abilities are extraordinary. She put us in touch with a woman's newspaper and gave us insightful advice as well.

All our practitioners were ready, willing, and most able to forge together, to hopefully make this first-time fundraiser a success. Pam thought of one more person who would truly make us complete. She suggested we have one vendor that would sell holistic items. Pam and I had met Jackie, owner of Trinity's Magickal Intentions, at another fundraiser in a nearby town. We were both impressed with her handmade creations, including jewelry, oils, candles, and more. Pam's gifted intuition guided her to ask Jackie to participate. Jackie, in addition to being a craftsman, also has intuitive abilities and graciously accepted. We were all ready to roll up our sleeves and set the wheels in motion.

We all pitched in to get the word out about our event. Jeff posted it on his website. That was the place to go to see our pictures, read our bios, and preregister. Flyers were posted throughout town and copies were given to local businesses. Pam had signs made and also made many herself. We drove around town putting them up. Pam and Jeff wrote articles for local newspapers. Filomena had a connection with a woman's paper, so our event had a write up there. Denise's employee used social media to get the word out. Our flyers were distributed at other Baird House events.

One local business owner, Mary, who loves our community and helps all causes, really went above and beyond. If you are ever in Millstone Township, New Jersey, please stop in for truly delicious Italian food and genuine hospitality at Vesuvio's Pizza Nicks Place. Mary's husband, Nick, started that wonderful establishment when there were only farms and open land. He built up his pride and joy and all his family members were a part of it. Sadly, he passed away unexpectedly. His son, Frank, has done an amazing job, continuing to expand the business with many innovative ideas that have added to their success.

Mary had contacted me for a medium reading before the event. She was hoping to hear from her beloved Nick. He immediately came through loud and clear! When he mentioned the peach trees, Mary said she knew instantly that it was him. He used his humor to make her laugh and smile, just as he did when he was alive. He gave many validations and answered questions. Mary's son and daughter were also at the reading and he gave them messages, too.

Mary was so happy to be able to connect; she wanted to do something special, to return the favor and help our cause. She put our flyer on the back of her mailer — one that goes out to THOUSANDS of households. Mary didn't stop there. She was so grateful; she put our flyers on the pizza boxes so that every take-out customer saw it. We can't thank you enough, Mary and Frank! Thanks to you too, Nick, from above!

Advertising was only one aspect of our event. There were plenty of others, numerous details, and countless hours that our group put in. It was so much more than any of us imagined, and we are psychics! WE DON'T KNOW EVERYTHING!

Although, as you and I both know, something we can all pretty much count on: SHIT HAPPENS!

It first started when Kathy called me to say she had a dilemma because her best friend was having a 100th birthday party for her mom on the same day as the fundraiser. I said, "Kathy, that is a once-in-a-lifetime event, and all of your family is going. You *have* to go! Denise will be just fine reading on her own." That was easy; what hit the fan next was not.

With two weeks to go, Filomenia was not going to be able to participate due to personal reasons. Now we were faced with the dilemma of finding another reader on short notice. YIKES! I remembered someone Pam and I had both been read by. Her name is Donna Russo. We were quite impressed with her abilities. She had her own unique style of reading with several decks, sometimes five at a time! She also includes numerology in her readings. One of her specialties is soul drawings, using her artistic abilities. I quickly emailed Donna and asked if she could help us out. My spirit guide, Marissa, must have taken pity on me and made sure Donna would say yes. The stars aligned, and Donna, who would use her tarot card reading skills, became part of our team.

My instincts told me we needed an additional medium since being down one would put us at a disadvantage. I looked to Jeff to bail us out again. Remember, Jeff is like a jack of all trades and can also do mediumship. Not only was he going to offer Reiki services at the fundraiser, but would offer his phenomenal medium abilities, too! Once again, I have to say, "Thank God for Jeff!"

The day of reckoning was upon us and we were ready to roll. I have to give a shout out to co-organizer Pam, my brother Bill, sister-in-law Fran, President of the Baird House Pat, esteemed members of the non-profit: Diane and Debbie, and friend to us all, Jimmy, for helping us. They each had a significant part in making sure the event ran smoothly.

We didn't know how many clients would be walk-ins. Some of the clients prepaid through Jeff's website, so we knew about them. Again, WE DON'T KNOW EVERYTHING! Can you guess what happened? We had an excellent turnout! People were lined up at the door and we had a steady stream throughout the day. Even though it was a rainy day, the weather didn't stop people from showing up. This may sound like a cliché, but for all the "blood, sweat, and tears," OUR PSYCHIC FUNDRAISER WAS A SUCCESS!

My intuition tells me that it was a mixture of assorted advertising and help from our dear departed loved ones. I must include all the readers' spirit guides and angels who helped to orchestrate as well. One last group to "seal the deal" were the spirits from the house itself. The room I read in was where a little girl had died. I felt her presence and "just knew" she was happy to help me connect to my client's passed loved ones. Some of my fellow readers also felt their particular Baird House spirit's helping hand. I give my heartfelt thanks to the living and non-living who made the psychic fundraiser a winning combination!

Chapter 18
Chance Encounter or Not

There is one client in particular who gave me many referrals. I *definitely* want to thank her! It's kind of funny how I met Beth. I had gone to a winery in a nearby town because I'd heard they had a ladies' night with different events. I asked the manager if she would be interested in having a medium or tarot card reader featured at one of the events. The manager said she had people she used and didn't need anyone else. Another lady was standing next to me. As soon as she heard what the manager said, she chimed in and said, "I've had them read me and those readers aren't any good!"

I looked at her, smiled, and said, "Well, I'm good!" She looked at me and asked if I had a card. I gave her one and left. I didn't think much more about it, but when I did, I got a good chuckle out of it. I enjoyed her brashness.

A few months later, she called me. We tried to coordinate a date, but it just didn't work out. She called me again, and we came up with a date and time that worked for us both. Timing is everything! When I first read for Beth, she didn't say much at all. She was more of the skeptical type. Her father came through for her and gave her several validations, although she was waiting for one in particular. Her father answered, "I'm no trained monkey!"

Beth's daughter was more of a believer. She validated some messages for Beth that came through. Beth's daughter also had a reading and was happy with hers.

I was surprised when people called to set up parties and they said Beth referred them. Beth became more of a believer, or maybe she wanted to see what other people thought of me.

I am very appreciative and grateful to Beth, her daughter, and her father, because word of mouth is the best compliment. It is also the best free advertising! Keep it coming!

You just never know what a chance encounter may bring. My original intent was to do readings at the winery. That didn't work out, but it sure did with Beth.

You may have one intention, but the universe may have another for you. So, sometimes just go with the flow. You never know where it may lead you.

Chapter 19
Teach

A woman I knew told me she gave classes at a community college. She had gotten some clients because of it and suggested I might want to try it. Since I had been an adjunct professor and enjoyed teaching, I figured I would give it a try. I had created accounting classes; I could create tarot card classes, too.

Continuing education classes are non-credit courses that students choose and are typically more enjoyable. That's where my tarot card class was offered. My introductory accounting class was a credit course. Most of the students had to be there because it was mandatory. I tried my best to have some fun with accounting. I know you are thinking:

accounting + fun = an oxymoron.

I discovered that teaching is one of my passions. I guess it goes along with my passion for helping others. I love sharing knowledge, ideas, and experiences. I am a people person, so interactions are really a delight for me. I get a thrill each time I see the lightbulb go off for a student. You can see it on his or her face. The "ah ha, now I understand" is quite different than the look of bewilderment . . . the expression of "What the hell is she talking about?" When I see that look, I almost go into a frenzy trying to rack my brain as to how to get my message across. I want to connect and have the student understand. When I do, the satisfaction is complete.

Whatever your passion or passions are, try to teach someone else. I know it's not for everyone, but you may just surprise yourself.

The benefits can be profound. I know some people think that if they teach someone else, it takes away from them. They think it can create competition. I don't look at it that way. I believe we are all in this together and there is enough to go around. Take a different perspective and see if it fits.

Speaking of teaching, let me tell you about Kerry. She ran the Continuing Education program at a local community college and hired me to teach classes there. I sure hit the jackpot with her! Kerry loves all types of psychic phenomena. She has great intuition herself, but started her own business, Soul Purpose Yoga & Wellness. She loved the idea of a tarot card class being offered at the college. When I met her, I gave her a tarot card reading and she was impressed. She immediately said she wanted me to have a party at her house. I have since done quite a few private readings and parties for her. I have taught more tarot card classes, too. Kerry has been so encouraging. She has given me many referrals and ideas to expand my business. We also did some events together where she sold homemade products and I did readings. Here's a heartfelt thanks to you, Kerry!

CHAPTER 20
Small World

Kerry was also instrumental in helping Artie Hoffman and I cross paths again.

I saw on Facebook that Artie would be participating at a holistic expo in a town nearby. I felt an urge to book a reading with him and I did. The expo was scheduled to be held in a couple of weeks. Kerry and I set a date to meet and discuss her helping me with marketing. That is one area where I am truly lacking and one in which she truly excels.

We got together and she gave me some ideas. She also explained how she helped a psychic medium, Artie, host a show on Facebook on Sunday nights. Kerry took the calls and Artie answered the questions.

I was shocked to hear this! "You know Artie?" I asked. She said she knew him and had been hosting the show with him for quite a while. "Wow," I said. "Small world."

It was what she told me next that really made my hair stand up! "I have been talking to Artie about you and how good you are with readings," Kerry said. "He said he would like to book a reading with you."

"Are you kidding me?" I asked. "I just booked a reading with him at the holistic expo. Why would he want a reading with me? He's an expert with readings and I'm still a novice compared to him." Remember, I had been a student in one of his classes. She said he had an issue and he wanted to discuss it. Sometimes it's hard for him to read for himself. I've got to admit, this blew my mind.

True to his word, Artie called me. He laughed about me booking him and he wanted to book me. We decided it would be best if he came to my house; he would read me and then I would read him. I wouldn't have to go the expo.

Artie's reading for me was superb. In true Artie fashion, he told jokes, gave insight into my future, relayed messages from my deceased mother-in-law, and provided with me with a bit of a therapy session . . . all rolled into one reading! It is quite an experience to be read by Artie.

Artie was impressed with my reading for him and encouraged me to keep working with my talents. He felt that one day there might be an opportunity to work on a party or project together and was looking forward to it. I am grateful to Artie for his words of encouragement.

Gratitude is something we need to focus on. We can't do everything alone. Stop and reflect on who has helped you along your journey. I bet that when you really stop to think about it, there are more people than you first thought of. I believe that the universe puts people in our paths for a reason. Some are good and some are bad, yet we learn lessons from them all. Now take the next step and contact them, whatever your preference may be. I'm old fashioned and still like to call people or, better yet, see them face to face. The younger generation may want to text or put something on Instagram. Whatever your choice, be sure to thank those people who did something for you, whether it was something big or small. They will be happy you did and so will you. It's a true win-win situation.

CHAPTER 21
Maria

I first met Maria when I gave her a medium reading. She became a mentor for me, although it didn't start out that way. During her reading, she said almost nothing. Sometimes I look for validation with a simple yes or no. I'll also ask if what I'm saying makes sense. Maria gave me practically nothing; my self-doubt started rearing its ugly head. I thought I must have been way off track. She didn't even change her expression. As I was closing her reading, I was afraid that she wasn't happy. I thought that I must not have hit on anything, but when I finished, what she said nearly knocked me off my chair! I'm psychic, but I definitely didn't see what was coming.

"I can't believe what you just told me! she exclaimed. "I *did* lose a baby girl. I know she sends me signs. What you said about my husband and my sister are all true. This is amazing!"

You could have knocked me over with a feather! I was amazed she said that to me! I asked her why she didn't validate the messages during her reading. She said she was in a state of shock, which left her speechless. I was glad she finally got her voice back. Consequently, my self-doubt was kicked to the curb.

Maria contacted me to do a medium party, but it didn't work out. Time passed and she contacted me again and asked if I could do a medium party at her house. This time it worked out. When she showed me to the room that I would be reading in, I had another shock. Maria is a Reiki Master. Her room had a Reiki table and all holistic paraphernalia. I didn't know that about her; she hadn't told me. Maria had healing and psychic abilities. We had something in common because she also helped people and enjoyed doing so.

Maria performed Reiki on me, which I definitely needed, and I gave medium readings to her. Maria's grandparents adored her, and she felt the same way about them. They came through in readings along with a woman who was like a "second mother" to her. These people meant the world to her and she was grateful to me for bringing them through and giving their messages. I discovered that I wasn't the only one who could bring through messages. Maria would give me messages while performing Reiki on me. Not all Reiki masters can do that.

Maria is blessed with this special talent. Her spirit guides and angels give her messages about all different kinds of issues for the people she works on. They are not her clients since she does not take any money. She performs Reiki out of the kindness of her heart. I am forever grateful to her because every one of the messages she gave me was something I needed to hear.

Maria told her friends and family, some of whom lived quite a distance away, about my abilities. She suggested that I give phone readings. I hadn't thought about that before, but said I would give it a try. I wasn't sure if my medium ability would work over the phone. To the delight of my newfound clients and myself, it worked! Sometimes you just have to take a leap of faith and try something. Once again, Maria was responsible for helping me.

As our friendship progressed, she started giving me advice on how to get more exposure for my abilities. I was still hesitant to fully come out of the psychic closet. She encouraged me to start a Facebook page and put myself on Instagram. That would definitely put me on display. Maria helped me find the courage inside myself to show the world this psychic part of me. She guided me to the cliff.

I took it one step further and exposed myself in a way that many people find quite natural. I'm a private person and not one to "let it all hang out." Maria encouraged me to take that leap of faith. As Tom Petty sang, I was "free-falling" into a new realm. I became hopeful and worthy of acceptance once I allowed my psychic abilities to be known to friends, colleagues, and clients.

Chapter 22
Facebook

Compared to Instagram, Facebook was the tougher of the two in my mind because I knew more people who were on it. I am technologically challenged; ask my children, and they will nod in full agreement. My son, Sean, helped me with Instagram and to my delight, it wasn't as challenging as I thought. That was definitely not the case with Facebook.

Sean helped me with that as well, or should I say, created it practically all by himself on the technical end. I simply helped by telling him what to write and which pictures to use for my Phyllis Mitchell page. One night, we sat down together and did just that. I finally had my own Facebook page for the entire world to see. Wow!

The next morning, I called Maria to see if she saw my page. I was shocked by her response. She said she couldn't find me. How could that be possible? My husband found me the night before. I called another friend, and she said the same thing. I just couldn't believe it!

I told Sean and we tried to get on my page, but found a message instead: "Your Facebook page has been disabled." We didn't understand why. Sean sent a message to Facebook and we waited for about a week before sending another. However, there was no response. I'm not blaming Facebook in any way, but I have a theory as to why my page didn't work at first. I can sum it up in one word: TIMING.

I have learned that while I may have a timeframe I believe works well, the universe is not always on the same page. Get it . . . page? Page? Facebook page. Ok, enough of that!

Sean tried a couple of different things to get me up and running but to no avail. Then miraculously, my Facebook page worked! The day it worked was on the twelfth. This is very significant since my sister's birthday was on the twelfth. Pat uses the number twelve in various ways to help me or just point out that she is around. You can call it coincidence; however, I just know it was my sister. I have seen it happen plenty of times. Maybe you have seen a particular number show up frequently, or a particular time on the clock or your watch. Think about it.

I'd also like to point out that our deceased loved ones have some type of connection (get it!) with electricity, technology, etc. Maybe your lights go on and off, or the TV turns on or off by itself. Maybe something strange happens with your computer that you just can't rationally explain. Think about it.

I do not really understand how spirits can manipulate such things, but like I said, I do not understand technology in the first place. I turn on my computer, TV, or cell phone, and they work. I don't have a clue as to how and, to be honest, I don't feel the burning desire to understand either. I'm just satisfied with their working condition.

Once my Facebook was up and running, some people started asking for friend requests. One name seemed familiar, but I wasn't sure about the last name because there was no picture on the account. Then the name dawned on me. I was quite certain that it was Carol, the woman I wrote about earlier, who was an excellent tarot card reader whom I just loved! Here was the issue — SHE IS IN THE SPIRIT WORLD!

I had to find out if that was her last name. I asked my friend Penelope. She didn't know, but loves a good mystery and is awesome about finding information. I wouldn't have thought of this, but it immediately came to her. She said she would look up the obituaries and see if it was, in fact, Carol's last name. You guessed it — it was! In my mind, I knew that Carol had helped me with Facebook and approved of what I was doing. She still wanted to be my friend! Somehow, from the spirit world, she friended me on Facebook. She still wanted to connect with me, and nothing was stopping her!

I was clueless as to how she was able to manipulate Facebook. As I said, understanding stuff like that is not important to me. Maybe it is important to you, and you can find someone to explain how she did it. Perhaps you or someone you know may have had that same experience, too. If so, please contact me because I would love to know!

People in the living, who knew I had psychic abilities, friended me on Facebook. I was hoping that people in the living that didn't know I had psychic abilities would friend me. Taking the steps to be on social media has worked for me because some of those unknowing people, and their friends, did friend me. You know how that goes. In addition, people were supportive. That was such a warm, welcoming feeling for me.

My post read:

> *Whether you know me as an accountant, financial literacy presenter, writer, psychic medium, tarot card reader or some of the above or all, I am me. The right and left side of my brain are either called upon independently or simultaneously. The common thread is: HELPING PEOPLE*

For some people, to show oneself in a different light can be too overwhelming to go it alone. You may want to find someone to help, or someone may just find you. Sometimes a friend, mentor, or both, may be the answer to your prayers. Maria, *mi amiga*, was mine. I can't thank her enough!

Chapter 23
Lessons

Sadly, gratitude is not in everyone's vocabulary. One woman I read for at a party didn't like who came through for her. One spirit was her former mother-in-law. You may be thinking, *Ok, I can't blame her.* However, this woman was disrespectful, even after hearing an insightful and caring message from her former mother-in-law. She just couldn't wait to move on.

Another spirit, a high school friend, who also had positive messages for her, came through. She became even more irritated and took her wrath out on me. She spoke condescendingly and the negativity dripped like boiling blood from her mouth. At that point, I wanted to stop, but something kept me going and kept me from saying that I didn't want to be treated like that.

Her grandmother came through. She had important messages for her, but my client just didn't want to listen. I said I couldn't control who connected, but it seemed like the spirits had meaningful messages for her.

This woman didn't take it well and implied that I just wasn't good. I didn't bring through who she wanted. She told me to tell her a specific thing she was thinking. When I told her that I didn't work that way, she said I was getting defensive. I felt like she was ready to battle me. It seemed in her mind, she had her ammunition ready. It was as if she was conveying, "See, you can't connect with the person I wanted, and you can't come up with the thought I was thinking."

I got a message at that point from her grandmother. I told the woman, "I can only relay the messages I am given from spirit. Right now, I will tell you, in her exact words, what your grandmother is relaying to me: "BRAT." You should have seen the look on her face. If looks could kill, I'd be dead! I told her truthfully, "I am only repeating your grandmother's message." There were three minutes of the fifteen left, but I wasn't going to be insulted or ridiculed any longer. I responded in a matter-of-fact tone, "I am ending this reading now. There is no need to pay me. I don't want your money. I will not email you your reading. Please tell the next woman I am ready for her. Thank you."

The next woman was the hostess of the party and my last person to read. She told me she was sorry for her co-worker's behavior. She said her co-worker could be difficult at times. I told her there was so much negativity around her. Some of the messages dealt with that particular issue for her. The spirits were trying to be helpful. Unfortunately, the co-worker would have none of it.

The hostess wanted to pay me for her co-worker's reading, but I told her, "No, thank you." She said maybe this was a lesson for me to learn. I agreed, we all have lessons to learn in life and this was certainly one for me. Lesson 1: Not everyone is willing to accept some facts about themselves and yet are very willing to place blame on another. Lesson 2: Believe in your own abilities, even when others don't.

These lessons gave me a "thicker skin." As I think about it now, I realize I am thankful for that experience, even though it was quite uncomfortable at the time. You may also benefit from those lessons, which can apply to anyone no matter who they are or what they are doing. There will be people who are negative, but we can't let that bring us down. Stay on the positive side and treat them as you wish they would treat you. Yes, take the higher ground. Don't get insulted. Realize we can't please everyone. That is hard for me since I am such a people pleaser. Maybe you are, too. Shake off the negative energy and put on your positive posture.

Most readings have a very positive effect on my clients. The feeling of connecting with passed loved ones can be a joy like no other. It allows clients to be with, feel, experience, hear, acknowledge, talk to, and listen to their deceased loved one. The spirit's essence comes through and validations are given. This brings comfort to my clients, knowing it is truly their departed loved one. The love they shared in life, is rekindled once again.

CHAPTER 24
Personalities

Personalities also come through in readings. I just love when spirits are funny! I guess it's because I enjoy people who are funny. I always enjoyed going to comedy shows and watching comedians on TV. I don't like to have favorites, but Robin Williams, a true genius, is my favorite — hands down. Perhaps, one day, I will connect with him; you just never know.

I type messages from spirits in my readings and, at times, will also ask my client if they would like to ask one or more questions. During the process, sometimes the spirit's humor comes through in a question or a message. Here are a few examples from various readings.

Question: "Do you talk to me?"

Answer: "I have a bullhorn and I'm yelling in your ear!"

Question: "Are you with the old crew?"

Answer: "Are you kidding me? The old crew — they didn't make it to heaven! I did!"

Question: "Why don't you show yourself to Phyllis?"

Answer: "I don't show my face to Phyllis because if I do, she will fall in love with me!"

Message: "All right already. Let's get this show on the road. Yes, I love to see her (my client) laugh. I can even make her pee her pants. Want to see? Only kidding!"

Message: "Lots of fun, adventure and romance on the horizon for you. If he wants you to take a trip with him, like Nike says, just do it! Don't worry; I won't be watching you all the time; you know what I mean."

There are some humorous messages that could be classified as "morbid humor," a phrase used by one of the spirits. Hopefully you enjoy some of the humor and get a chuckle or two out of them. My clients and I certainly did! One spirit sprinkled these snippets.

Message: "I always had a funny side, but at the same time I could be dead serious — get the pun?"

"I looked pretty damn good for being dead."

"On a serious note, I miss my kids like hell. Oops — didn't mean to say that, morbid humor."

"I can't tell you what I do here, it's top secret. If I tell you, I have to kill you. Get it — more morbid humor."

"Yes, I am a jokester and that thankfully hasn't changed. Tell my mom and dad I won't see them anytime soon and that's the good news."

"Always keep humor close. Yes, it's cliché, but laughter is the best medicine. Didn't work for me but think it will for you.

Again, I can't help saying morbid humor."

Here's some more "morbid humor" from another spirit.

Message: "I am here! I want you to understand I love it here. It is unbelievable. I didn't even have to pay to get in!"

> "Wait until you die — there will be thousands coming to your funeral. If the animals could come, they would, too. Could you imagine? The cats and dogs dressing up in suits walking in paying their respects!"

Clichés and expressions also pop up during readings. Clichés, even though we may not want to admit it, are ways to make a point.

One spirit was known for using them in her everyday life and death didn't stop her. She sure used plenty to validate it was her! She had seven of them all in one reading! Okay, I just can't help myself, "Lucky number seven!"

> Message: "Stay the course."
>
> "You have big shoulders."
>
> "A word to the wise."
>
> "Shit or get off the pot."
>
> "You can bet your bottom dollar."
>
> "Sink or swim."
>
> "Watch your p's and q's."

One male spirit gave three expressions. He was "short and sweet!"

> Message: "Take the plunge."
>
> "Rome wasn't built in a day."
>
> "Don't take any wooden nickels."

Some messages aren't as lighthearted. They don't pull any punches and make you want to say "OUCH!" Please read these snarky messages that came through from spirit. Even from beyond, loved ones can still dole it out!

> Message: "Aunt Kay coming through. I should have been on the cover of a magazine. What she is wearing today, you won't see her on the magazine. I am elegant, had money in my pocket and had a ring on my finger. I don't see a ring on her finger. Yes, I could be crass, but held my head high."
>
> Message: "Aunt CT coming through loud and clear and I'm not holding back! I'm a straight-shooter. What's up with your man? You have to put a leash on him. He's flitting all over the place. He's a talker, likes the ladies, flirtatious. Yes, he better keep it in his pants. If not, kick him in the ass and out the door. Give him a warning from me."

These are actual quotes from readings I have given. As they say, "You can't make this stuff up!" These examples are proof to me that the personality, the "essence" of a person lives on.

CHAPTER 25
Serious Significances

Spirits also give very serious messages. Some are about relationships. Here is an excerpt from one reading that the dad wanted to have his daughter think about. These wise words can be read for all of us to ponder. I've also included an excerpt from a grandmother giving her granddaughter a glimpse into her future relationship.

Dad:

When you love, love deeply and honestly. Expect nothing less in return. Love is a two-way street, a give and take. Respect is immensely important. Without it, there truly is no love, no real love from the heart and soul. Think about these words, reflect and draw your own conclusions. A love that is pure will blossom. A love that is not, will wither away. I wish you all the best that the world has to offer. Choose wisely.

Grandmother:

You will meet someone who you can shower your love with. Focus on one, but still plenty of love to go around. Guess what? That special someone will love animals; you wouldn't settle for less. You will meet this person by accident in a way. It is not planned. I like that it will take you by surprise. It will be a whirlwind romance. Things will go quickly. There will be babies of course. You are a nurturer to start, so it makes perfect sense. I will be at the wedding and your mother will be beside herself. I can just picture her beaming, smiling from ear to ear.

I receive plenty of messages about a client's health or the health of a living loved one. A theme, closely related, is stress. One mother gave advice to her "good boy," even though he is in his sixties! A grandmother was worried about her daughter and asked her granddaughter to give her a message. Another mom had a warning for her son and relayed the message to his wife.

One mother:

I want to warn you about your health. You are not worried, but I am. I'm not kidding on this one. Please stop burning the candle at both ends because it will truly catch up with you and I don't want to see anything happen. Forewarned is forearmed. Get yourself to a doctor. There's stress all around you. Promise me this. Now that's a good boy.

Grandmother:

Your mom has some health issues she needs to address. I'm not trying to scare you. Make sure she goes for a mammogram, Pap smear, regular woman things. Keep checking woman things. It's better to be safe than sorry.

Another mother:

I know Tom has tears in his eyes. I see them and it breaks my heart. In time he will feel better, but now it's hard for him to accept. Yes, his stress level is starting to creep off the charts. He needs to relax, relax, relax. He is being pulled in so many directions, his head is spinning. He is wearing his shoes out. Please tell him to put on a coat, too. It can be bitter cold, and he thinks he can't feel it, but he will.

Many spirits have the same idea about relieving stress: VACATION!

One man's message was:

Live your life fully. Don't have regrets and there is no time like the present. So, go on vacation! Just go and don't think twice.

If you want to go on a cruise, go ahead. If you want to be a landlubber, you have my blessing for that. The choice is yours to make, so make it.

One grandmother advised:

You are going to be going on a boat soon. Relax and enjoy! A short trip will be presented. Don't hesitate, say YES!

Some spirits, in their messages, give personal explanations about who helped them cross over or who they will help cross over. Some even give us a glimpse behind the "veil" and let us in on what they are doing. Wow, just writing it gives me chills!

One brother relayed to his sister:

Dad was there to help me cross over. It wasn't scary. Actually, it was truly beautiful. The sense of peace is truly amazing. When it is your time, and not right now, God knows when, you will see my smiling face to help you. I will hold out my hand and then hold you close. I'll give you a brotherly hug to have you feel all my love.

One friend to a friend:

Your soul has such endless boundless love. For that, you are rewarded in the physical world, but you will be even more so, in the spiritual world, when you pass. Don't worry, it won't be any time soon, but I will be waiting for you with open arms. A true blessing you are.

One brother to another:

I am in heaven, so I am at peace. I see what goes on with everyone. I also have a job that keeps me busy and I just love it. I help young children cross over. They are so young, and I help guide them. Please tell Mom and Dad this. It will make them feel a little better.

There are numerous topics that come up in messages from loved ones. One message about love that consistently comes through, although stated in different ways, is definitely not a cliché.

LOVE IS ETERNAL.
LOVE NEVER DIES.
LOVE IS EVERLASTING.
LOVE YOU FOREVER AND FOREVER.
LOVE IS THE ANSWER.

These messages about love, along with asking the living person to continue living and find peace, are dominant themes in readings.

Here is an excerpt of one woman's reading, connecting with her son with these powerful messages. It captures themes of love, and the loved one left on earth, to continue living. It's important for me to let you know that while I was typing the messages, my body had chills and there was so much emotion running through me. I also cried during most of it.

Mom, I can't describe how much I love you. You couldn't have done anything better for me. I appreciate every, and I mean every single thing you have ever done for me. And believe me there were plenty. I cherish ***each*** *and* ***every*** *moment I had with you. I know you feel me around you. Yes, it is me. Believe me when I tell you. I touch your face. I watch you at night; night-time seems to be the hardest time for you. I see you look at my picture but please realize I am with you. Feel my presence. Expand your mind and realize I will never leave you. I know your thoughts. I see your actions. We still bond Mom. That will never be broken.* ***Love never dies.*** *Mom, please listen to me when I tell you. I am happy here. I am working. I talk to children and you know this makes me happy. I am at peace.*

I too pray for you to ***find peace for yourself.*** *When you do, my heart will rest. Please give your heart to me by helping yourself. That is what I* ***truly*** *want for you. Please Mom, you never denied me before, please don't now. Please allow yourself to* ***find peace*** *and give your love to others who are also so deserving. Mom, do you hear me? Do you understand Mom, what I'm trying to say?* ***Mom, you have your life to live.*** *There is so much more you can do. Please Mom, please start doing. That would mean the world to me. You know you mean the world to me. I want to see you happy and smiling. You are truly a beautiful woman both inside and out. I feel truly grateful that you are my Mom.* ***Please Mom, you must live, and you must live to the fullest.*** *Please Mom, don't be a shell of yourself. There is so much vibrancy you always had. Please Mom, shine again. I want to help you with this. Mom, will you promise me that you will do what I ask? Mom, please don't try, please say you will. Thank you, Mom. You don't know how happy that makes me feel.* ***I love you Mom. Mom, I always loved you and I always will. Now it's your time to live. Mom, I mean really live.***

Love you forever and forever.

Chapter 26
Signs

Signs are another familiar way to get people to realize their passed loved ones are around them. Birds are especially common signs. In my case, blue jays are from my father and cardinals from my sister. I guess my father wanted to stick with his bird theme and sends feathers!

My mother sends dimes. She collected them throughout her life, so it would be appropriate for her to leave them around to be found. Our loved ones leave coins in washing machines, dryers, parking lots, counters, and chairs, just to name a few. My Uncle Tony sends nickels. I must be honest; I'm not sure why. I just know they are from him. My sister sends pennies . . . "pennies from heaven" and I think she wanted to distinguish herself from my mother. My mother-in-law knew about what my mother, sister, and uncle sent. I'm guessing that's why she chose quarters to send to us. Although my niece pointed out another reason: my brother-in-law collected state quarters and got my mother-in-law to do it, too.

While I was in the process of writing a eulogy for my mother-in-law, Arlene, she came into my mind, and I heard the song *I Just Called to Say I Love You* by Stevie Wonder. I loved my mother-in-law and felt blessed to have had a good relationship with her. We enjoyed shopping, going out to lunch, sharing our feelings, and laughing together. We loved talking on the phone and catching up on all the happenings in the family. She, like me, enjoyed going to psychics and mediums. A reading was a favorite gift to give her. Arlene and I went to quite a few together and eagerly discussed what "came through."

When she was in the hospital, my husband and I would visit Arlene frequently, although my sons were not always able to. I made sure they would talk to her on the phone and each one of us would say "I love you" to her. She wasn't always able to answer us back, but after she passed, I feel she wanted to acknowledge what we did for her. The song allowed her to return the favor and say it to us.

Pat sends the song *Ain't No Mountain High Enough* by Diana Ross. My niece, Danielle, first heard it and associated it with her mother. Danielle told our family about it. Several members of our family hear that song and immediately think of Pat. The words of the song give her message. Pat also sends me the song *We Are Family* by Sister Sledge. The words of the song definitely relate to the two of us. The song *Under the Boardwalk* by The Drifters is the one song my family associates with my father. There is an inside family joke about that one. Sorry, can't share.

Has a song started playing that reminds you of someone who has passed? Are there any pennies or dimes that cross your path? Have you seen someone who looks almost exactly like a passed loved one? Do lights go on and off by themselves? Does the phone ring yet there is no one there? Do you start searching for something you know was in one place, but you find it in another? If not, be on the lookout! These random occurrences may not be so random at all. Sometimes it is simply a matter of **realizing** your passed loved one is responsible for sending you those signs.

Chapter 27
Website

I believe some of my passed loved ones helped me with my website. I had been thinking of having a website created to give me more exposure. Another reason was to put myself in the twenty-first century; my sons always teased me about this. I knew hiring someone to create a website could be expensive. I hadn't earned much revenue from readings, so the accountant in me wouldn't justify the expense. I am a member of the New Jersey Society of CPAs, an excellent organization that helps its members in a variety of ways.

The New Jersey Society of CPAs sent out an email about Monmouth University looking for small businesses that were in need of a website. One of the professors wanted to give her students "hands-on experience" developing websites. Sometimes, textbook examples don't do justice and can't compare to the actual experience. Having taught, I couldn't agree more.

The icing on the cake of the professor's offer was that the students would create a website for free! I couldn't believe my luck! I immediately thought, "Sign me up!" At first, I was a bit nervous and wondered if the professor would be open to my "different kind of business." I emailed the professor and wrote that I had gotten the information from the New Jersey Society of CPAs. I explained that I had a small accounting practice, as requested, but that was not the business for which I wanted a website. I wanted one for my intuitive readings. I am grateful to the professor who was open-minded and said it would be fine.

I started wondering about my good fortune. I had wanted a website for my new business, but revenues wouldn't support it.

Out of the blue, this email miraculously appeared. It wouldn't cost me anything, and the professor approved my business so easily. My intuition had given me the answer; my parents worked their magic from above. A phenomenal gift! Thank you, Mom and Dad!

I had the pleasure of working with two extremely talented students. They are very intelligent, creative, savvy, professional, and courteous. I could sing their praises on and on. One student, who was able to spend more time with me, went above and beyond. She is also a professional photographer and suggested I get a new picture of myself. I had her take it and used it on my website; however, she would not take any money. Every time I had a question or wanted a change made, she was accommodating and punctual. She definitely deserved an A for her abilities and customer service. I was extremely pleased with how the website turned out, as was the professor. Both students received an A for the course, while I was provided with an excellent website. It was a win-win all the way around.

I kept that website for about a year, but it had one drawback; it was not user-friendly. They created it using code. As I have mentioned, I am technically challenged. So, with the help of my friend, Penelope, and my son, Sean, we created a new and improved website. The website still had some features from the old one. However, one important difference, was that I could actually make changes in the new one. That is quite an accomplishment for me! When you get a chance, check it out at www.readingsbyphyllis.com. I appreciate all kinds of comments: the good, bad, and of course, the ugly, too!

Chapter 28
Skeptics

After hearing that particular story, you may believe, as I do, that my deceased parents helped me. Conversely, you may rationalize that it was only a coincidence that I was able to get a free website. I feel there are different kinds of people: believers, skeptics, and nonbelievers. There are also levels of degrees in each category. The following is an experience I had with a skeptic.

I was giving readings at a local bookstore. I don't get many male clients, but that day I got one. He came in, sat down, and in no uncertain terms, immediately told me, "I am a skeptic. The only reason I came was because of a friend." What a great way to set the stage.

I told him there was a man who, I felt, wanted to connect with him. He told me that his uncle had passed away a week before. Immediately, his uncle gave me a message, "Yes, I sailed. You just check it out." I relayed this to my client.

My client looked at me and said that wasn't true. His uncle responded, "Now you wouldn't call me a liar. I pulled no punches. I'm a straight-shooter!" It was interesting how his uncle immediately responded to his response to me. My client did admit that his uncle was not a liar and, in fact, spoke his mind.

His uncle said he liked shoes; however, my client said he had no idea about this. His uncle responded, "Ask your mother!" Again, it was as if they were having an actual discussion.

His uncle also said, "You are close to your cousin, and you know damn well who I am talking about; he is like a brother to you. Can you confirm this?" My client did confirm. His uncle continued, "Did you ever think in a million years I would be the type of person who would use a medium to connect with you?

No damn way. But here I am. Go figure!" My client confirmed this, too. His uncle stated, "Your mother was and always will be the apple of my eye. I will watch out for her through eternity. We were thick as thieves. Understand my meaning?" My client definitely understood. He told me his mother and uncle were twins and had a close relationship.

My client thanked me for my time and said he would speak with his mother about his reading. He was adamant about wanting his uncle to mention something about being a pilot. They both were and had that in common. Even though he could validate some of the messages his uncle gave, he was disappointed that aviation wasn't mentioned. It strengthened his conviction for being a skeptic. I got the feeling he came in as a skeptic and left the same way.

I emailed him his reading and to my surprise, he emailed me back rather quickly. His response shocked me on a few levels. This is what he sent:

Hi Phyllis,

Thank you for the copy of my reading. I did speak with my Mom, and must say that I was surprised to hear what she said and validated. . . Even though I am still a skeptic, after speaking with my Mom, it certainly did open my mind quite a bit. . . .

My uncle was an airline pilot by trade, like me. As such, the mentioning of a sailor confused me a lot, and you had almost completely lost me at that point. I had really thought if there was any sort of real connection, that flying, and aviation would have come through in the reading. Having said that, he had retired early due to medical reasons, and after I moved to the US, my Mom confirmed that he did take a significant interest into boating and sailing. Even to the point that he apparently, unbeknownst to me, had gotten all his boating/sailing licenses, including for bigger commercial ships. This is just absolutely shocking to me, but also interesting how you communicated about a fact that I was unaware of.

Another fact that my Mom was able to confirm was that he was definitely into shoes. Also, something I was unaware of. Not only that, he had recently had a conversation with my mom, about new shoes he got, which he really liked, but my mom wasn't too impressed with them, again showing he was into shoes.

My mom asked if he was at peace, but I told her that didn't come up directly. However, I did tell her that you thought he was funny and had joked a little bit with you, which is typically him. That made my mom happy to hear, with the assumption that he must be at peace if he can still be funny.

So even though my mind has opened quite a bit, I remain a skeptic, mostly because no aviation related matters had come through, which was really the main connection I had with my uncle. . . .

That is what he emailed me. So, my client is now a more open-minded skeptic? That's an oxymoron, but I'll take it! Again, there are levels of degree for believers, skeptics, and nonbelievers.

That proves to me that I am not picking up on the thoughts or memories of my clients. Isn't it ironic that a skeptic was involved for me to draw that conclusion? Some people think this is the explanation of how I get my messages. Clearly, my client didn't have a clue about his uncle's sailing or love of shoes. Perhaps this is additional proof; I really am getting messages from dead people!

In this case, I think my client's uncle wanted to connect with his sister, my client's mom. His uncle gave messages that almost forced him to talk to his mom. Sometimes, deceased loved ones will figure out a way to get their message across to the person it was intended for.

I understand part of the reason why a person can be a skeptic. I admit I am not 100 percent correct all the time. I don't know a psychic who is. That's the thing with readings. There are excellent psychics, but we are human beings, and no one is perfect. For example, I am familiar with baseball. My son Sean played, and my son Dean still does. We watch the Yankees quite a bit. The professional players are highly regarded and quite valuable for having high batting average scores.

Here's a little trivia for you, although if my statistics are off, it is not intentional! I Googled the highest batting average score of the season. "Ted Williams was the last hitter to hit at least .400 after finishing with a batting average of .406 in 1941." That means that when he was at bat, he hit about 40 percent of the time, meaning he didn't hit about 60 percent of the time. Remember, he has the highest average to date! In my opinion, there are a couple true role models in Yankees baseball whom I would also give VERY high marks for their moral character. Their batting averages are not as high as Ted's. Per Google:

Derek Jeter from 1995-2014 his overall season batting average is a .310

Aaron Judge from 2016-2019 (June) his overall season batting average is a .274.

Considering this, please do not judge me if I am not always 100 percent correct. I wish I could be right all the time for my clients, but it just can't be. Yet, skeptics will grab this bone and not let go. They will make a blanket assumption that psychics are wrong or go even further to say they are intentionally making everything up. Many theories circulate. My theory is that we have free will and there are different paths offered to us. A psychic sees one of the paths that may be the most likely, however, it is not a definite. A medium receives a message from a loved one about the client's future, yet it may not happen. I feel that sometimes the client goes off course and chooses another direction that is offered. Sound familiar? Remember though, this is a theory. You may have your own theory. Basically, we are humans and we are not perfect. Add in the element of free will and we just can't bat a thousand. Not even famous baseball players can!

Chapter 29
Attention Getters

I have another interesting story for you if you are up for it. Talk about a curveball! I have a phone for my CPA business. I was blow-drying my hair one day while watching TV. The business phone rang, and I saw a name come across the TV screen. It was one of my son's baseball coaches from several years ago. I thought that was strange for two reasons. One, the man hadn't been his coach for at least six or seven years, and two, I had never given him my business phone number. When coaches ask for contact information, I always give my cell phone number.

I just *knew* that the coach didn't actually call me. I had a strong feeling someone who had passed was responsible for the call. My business phone shows the name and phone number of the caller. I called his number back to see what was going on, but it was a strange busy signal. I tried another time, and the same thing happened. My husband suggested I take a picture of the name and number. Armed with those pictures, I felt I needed to stop by the coach's house and see what was going on. The next day I checked Facebook and I saw something posted from the coach's wife. I had never seen anything on Facebook from her before. The plot had thickened.

I got the feeling that someone who passed was trying to connect with the coach's wife and not him. Since I knew her, too, I decided to stop by her house and tell her what had happened. She was surprised, but said her husband had been having issues with his business phone. She said she wasn't a true believer, yet not a true disbeliever either. I'll call her a skeptic. She agreed to have me come back and do a reading for her.

It turns out, her neighbor with whom she was quite friendly, connected during the reading. Her neighbor had died of cancer. She had messages for the coach's wife and, more importantly, had messages for her own children she had left behind. Here is an excerpt from the reading:

My kids were and still are my life. I pray with all my heart and soul they believe me that I came through. Please help them with this; it is not easy to just believe. Please let my kids know I love them with all my heart and soul. They may believe this or say it is just full of shit! Again, it's their choice to make. Family, faith and love is what they should focus on. Please relay that message to them. I will be forever, and I mean forever, grateful. God be with you always.

The coach's wife promised she would tell the children. She said she would give them my card to see if they would agree to see me in order to receive messages from their mom. This mom didn't jump through hoops, but phones to start the process of connecting. She figured out a way to connect with me, first through the coach and then through his wife, to get messages to her children. That's determination! I hoped and prayed her children were as determined to connect with her.

My prayers were answered five months later. Her daughter emailed me and wanted to set up an appointment. She thought it would be good for her sister to have a reading, too. On the day of the appointment, her sister couldn't make it, so her husband came instead. He considered himself like a son to her mom. They took turns being read while the other drove their four children around.

The determined mom relayed her true colors once again. Her messages were as if she was speaking right to them. She swore, gave blunt advice, and was mushy. In addition, she reminisced and made some predictions. Her effect on them was the same, they laughed and cried. Her daughter and son-in-law both loved that they were able to connect with her once again. Her son-in-law got an extra treat. He was thrilled he had been able to connect with two additional spirits who had made a strong impact on his life.

There was another woman, Janet, from my town who died. I knew her because we were both members of the Moms Club in our town. When I first moved to town, I joined to meet other moms and kids. Dean was three years old at the time. Janet had a son one year older than mine, another the same age as Sean, and a daughter who was the oldest.

Her daughter, Lindsay, would babysit my boys from time to time. We lost touch as our boys got older and we no longer belonged to the Moms Club. I was shocked to hear Janet had passed away.

Janet had an interesting way of getting my attention; she used LinkedIn. LinkedIn will periodically send out emails asking if you know a person with whom you haven't connected. I had never gotten a request from her when she was living, but my belief is that she sent me one since she had passed. I felt she wanted me to connect with her loved ones.

I spoke about this to my friend who also knew Janet. My friend told me that Janet's daughter, Lindsay, and husband, John, had been quite distraught over her passing. She felt it could help comfort them to get a reading from me and offered to ask them if they would be interested.

Lindsay and John were very receptive to the idea and texted me to set up an appointment. I read for them both and Janet had many messages for them. Messages of hope were dominant. They were very emotional, crying tears of sadness and joy. It warmed their hearts and souls to hear from her.

Several months later, I read for Lindsay again, since I had gotten another LinkedIn request. That time of year was very special to Lindsay and Janet, which brought familiar memories. Through Lindsay's tears, her mom's messages brought her comfort. Lindsay wrote me a note explaining how she felt. "Our sessions together helped me deepen my spirituality, which it's something I have never had before. Ever since our reading, I have stopped blaming myself and questioning why, which is a huge burden lifted off my shoulders. You have helped me tremendously in my grief journey, and I am so grateful for that."

I have since gotten more emails from LinkedIn. When I do, I text Lindsay and she is always eager to get a reading. I have the feeling I will continue getting them.

These two spirits used methods of connection that are used in the physical world to get my attention. I followed through and allowed spirits to connect and give messages to their loved ones. I must hand it to them; sometimes spirits can be quite creative in how they reach out.

Chapter 30
On the Radio

One time, I had messages coming through at a neighbor's pool party. I had no intention of reading anyone there. I was there to talk, eat, and mingle.

I started talking to one woman whom I had met the previous year at one of my neighbor's parties. My neighbors are party people and I love them for it! They are also very caring neighbors in every sense of the word. The woman and I were having some girl-talk about her boyfriend. She asked me to talk to him and see if I got any vibes about him.

I went over and started talking to him. I immediately liked him! He told me his name was Andy Kin. I got a good vibe from him, a genuine sincerity. I felt he was talkative, interesting, sweet, kind, honest, and trustworthy. In my book, those are all good qualities to have in a boyfriend. We were talking for a while and then it hit me. Someone started giving me messages for him. I realized it was his deceased wife. She let me know she was thankful for all he did, taking care of her before she passed. She gave me the message that she had sent this particular woman to him so he would not be alone. She felt he deserved someone he could be happy with. I gave him all that information and some more. Andy was surprised that I had medium abilities, but he said he was a *believer.* He had experienced signs and other happenings to make him one.

Andy told me he volunteered at the radio station 89.7 WDVR and interviewed all kinds of people on the show *Let's Talk.* I received a message from someone to ask him if he would interview me. My question seemed to flow right out of my mouth!

Andy immediately said he would love to have me as a guest. He gave me his card and said to get in touch with him to pick a date. Wow! That came out of left field, but I guess I caught the ball!

I contacted Andy shortly after, but I didn't hear back. I gave it some time, but still didn't get a response. I got discouraged and let it go. After more time passed, I happened to mention it to my friend, Penelope. She insisted I contact him again. She is such a good friend, always giving me encouragement. He responded and set up a date close to Halloween. How appropriate!

Andy's co-host, Claudine Wolk, texted me to set up a phone call, to learn more about me, and come up with some questions. We hit it off immediately! She loves all "psychic stuff" and is a big believer! We had other things in common, too. Claudine is also an accountant and enjoys writing. Unlike me, though, she had published a book already. I told her I was still working on mine. We chatted away and time flew by! I became less nervous and more excited about the interview, informing her that after my interview I would do a reading at the studio for her. She became excited as well!

October 28 rolled in and I was ready to make my first radio debut. I was happy to see the host again, such a wonderful man! Andy introduced me to Claudine and my vibe about her was right. In person, she was beautiful inside and out. Her bubbly nature was the cherry on top.

They explained a few procedures to me and gave me headphones. Once I put those on, I was ready to go, when the light went on. They had plenty of questions ready, yet a sense of peace came over me. I felt the universe had taken away any fear and allowed me to answer with grace and sincerity.

I was still writing this book at the time, so they said they would have me back when my book was published. I was thrilled to hear they wanted me back! It was also an incentive to finish this book.

After the interview, I did a medium reading for Claudine off the air. She was so thankful her father-in-law connected with her. He gave her plenty of messages and validations. She was excited to be able to share them with her husband. I also did a tarot card reading that highlighted some delicate family issues to be resolved. She was grateful the readings weren't on air. Claudine said she would discuss her experience with my readings. True to her word, the following week she happily did just that and was very complimentary. She called me and said she would send me a copy of the interview. As we chatted, she gave me advice about writing my book. She truly got the ball rolling and lit a fire under me to push forward with my book. In return, I helped her by giving her readings.

Chapter 31
Open Discussion

The benefits are endless when we reach out and help. Remember the Baird House event I wrote about earlier? We had a tricky tray there and a free medium reading was what I donated. A woman named Karin won. I called her a few days later and ended up doing a reading for her at her house. We started chatting afterward. Karin asked, "Wouldn't it be great to gather a group together and discuss different topics about intuition and share experiences?" I just loved her idea and totally agreed!

It took me some time, but that is exactly what I did. I thought of different people to invite to my house for what I called an "open discussion." Our first gathering included me, three other psychics (Denise, Kathy and Sal) and eight people whom I sensed had intuitive abilities. Some of the people didn't realize their own capabilities or were doubtful of them. Of those people, some were my clients. It is interesting how I seem to attract people for my readings who have abilities themselves.

I think it is the "teacher" in me who realizes the potential in a student and wants him or her to blossom. Some of the people who attended knew they had abilities but didn't know what to do with them. We had a nice mix of twelve people. Remember, twelve is a significant number for my sister. I think she worked her magic from above to get things started. Thanks, Pat!

We sat in my basement, which my husband had just finished. I am forever grateful to Mitch for his handyman talents. The basement came out perfect and we saved a ton of money not having to hire a professional.

Refreshments were served, introductions made, and we were off to a good start. I paired up people who didn't know one another in groups of two. I asked them to come up with three characteristics about each other by holding one another's jewelry, looking at that person, or getting a feeling. I also asked them to see if they could get any other information. They did just that and wrote things down. I wanted everyone to realize that they had intuition and it could be validated by a stranger.

I had them go around the room and relay what came to them. Their results were quite impressive! Some of them were simply amazed at what they could do. The teacher in me loved watching their astonished faces as their partners validated that what they said was true. I wanted to prove to them they could do it, and do it they did! The group blossomed and sweetly surprised themselves with their intuitive abilities. Smiles lit up the room; it was a joyful atmosphere. We were off to a good start. The Universe had indeed worked its enchanting ways.

Our discussion was such a wonderful encounter that we decided to gather at my house on a consistent basis. In the months ahead, various topics started popping up and various people offered their opinions and experiences. Presentations, along with meditations, were given by both me and others. There were some regulars, some people who only came once, and others who came and went. The mix of people and topics changed, but the exciting exercises and sharing of stories were always present. A newfound camaraderie was born in my basement!

One person, who I would like to highlight, is Lynn. She has excellent intuition. She is also quite a motivator! I was hesitant to put myself out there, so she gave me ideas about what to discuss and, after the meeting, was quite complimentary. Lynn is the type of person who makes you feel good about yourself and does so genuinely. Yet, she is humble about her own abilities. I look to her as a mentor and she continues to encourage and empower me. Thanks Lynn!

The open discussions fueled a place for learning, sharing, and caring. They lasted for several months and were quite successful. However, they were cut short. An event happened that changed nearly everything.

Chapter 32
Missing Person

My moral compass, once again, wants me to protect privacy. I will not reveal the name of the person missing, nor people close to the case. I will stay away from some of the specifics related to the case.

One soul I connected with gave me messages about a killer and their location, although the information was not as crystal clear as I would have hoped. Instead, there were bits of information that were like pieces to a puzzle. I felt a strong need to give the information I received to police, as I had done with the missing boy, Brandon. This person was missing, too. I wasn't exactly sure what would be done with the information, but in my heart, I felt it was the right thing to do.

I got the idea that I should discuss this missing person with others. I felt that letting different people who had good intuition give their input would be a better approach. We could combine messages, images, thoughts, signs, and feelings to help. I put the open discussion on hold. I narrowed down people from the open discussion to four and a new group was formed. We bonded and met frequently. We all felt the missing person was killed and had connected with each one of us to give information.

We each receive information differently. As you know, one way I get messages is through thoughts in my mind and I write or type them. I also "just know" things. Karin is very visual. She easily goes to another realm and connects to see visions. She has dreams, too. Suzanne, like Karin, is also visual. In addition, she "just knows" things. When the two of them were not together, they pinpointed the very same location where they thought the body was buried. That is pretty amazing! I had gotten a few details related to location, but nothing specific, like Karin and Suzanne. Not unlike me, they are in the process of realizing more about their abilities and working to expand them. Michele is very seasoned, with excellent intuitive abilities. She is visual, gets feelings, and "just knows." We rely on her to help guide us. She leads our meditations in order to open us up more to receiving information. She, truly, is a mentor to us all.

We looked forward to exchanging what we received, using our intuition. We were hoping to put our heads together to come to a resolution. However, we kept getting more pieces to the puzzle. Consequently, we gave some of our combined information to the police. Shortly after, the murderer was brought to justice by his own hand. The person, who we suspected to be the murderer, turned out to be the culprit.

Since the murderer didn't give location, it became our full focus. I spoke with a few of my intuitive friends outside of our group. I was hoping strength in numbers would bring us closer to solving the mystery. Sal, Bonnie, Lynn and Alexa (each written about earlier) explained their thoughts to me. They, too, got pieces of the puzzle. Some information was aligned with what our group came up with and some was different.

Time passed and we decided to contact people close to the case. We gave them the "pieces" that we all had received. However, more time passed and the person was still not found. Frustration agonizingly kicked in. One message that the missing person emphasized did ring clear throughout. The message was, "When the time is right, I will be found." So we tried to keep the faith that "timing is everything." Sure enough, that message was correct. The body was not discovered during a search, but was "randomly" found by people walking near it. Unfortunately, we were not correct regarding location. Other information we received and passed along rang true because the missing person relayed that information quite well to us.

It was bittersweet for the family. The negative was that their child had, in fact, been killed. The positive was that they had closure and their child could be laid to rest. The family also made sure their child's death would not be in vain. Good can come from evil. They created a foundation in honor of their child whose legacy will live on. Hope is part of their message.

Chapter 33
Hope, Help, Give

Hope is a treasure for the soul. I believe messages can also bring hope. Do you remember I wrote earlier about the party my Rutgers roommate gave in 2017? Sal and I had given readings to her guests. I gave a reading to one woman that made a lasting impression on her. She rode the roller coaster ride of infertility, which can be devastating during the low times. The reading I gave her relayed that her journey would not be an easy one, with many struggles ahead. Yet, I pleaded with her to not give up hope; it was going to happen for her. She would become a mom. However, it would not happen the way she envisioned it and in the time frame she expected. I told her to allow the universe to take over and her wish would come true.

I recently had the pleasure of seeing her and hearing her poignant story via a Zoom meeting. She told me that she and her husband had tried different methods of assistance with getting pregnant and none had worked. They felt tired and defeated. They eventually decided to try one of the most expensive methods, in vitro fertilization. Sadly, it was also unsuccessful. They were ready to give up. They were spent, both literally and figuratively.

However, a thought kept popping up in her mind about my reading. She and her husband decided to try one more time with in vitro fertilization. To their amazement and sheer delight, it worked! Even so, she had a long battle ahead to maintain the pregnancy. They both kept the faith, and a beautiful healthy baby girl was born.

The woman showed me her baby, who was fifteen months at the time of the Zoom meeting. I agreed with her; that precious, happy child is a true blessing. The woman cried and couldn't thank me enough for the words of encouragement I had given her. What a wonderful feeling for me that I could now share in her joy! I wanted her to understand that even though they were my words, I am a messenger. Those words of hope came from another source. While I was reading her tarot cards, messages came through that she was meant to hear. Hope helped to make her dream come true.

Hope is a treasure for the soul. I believe messages from spirits can also bring hope. Allow it to be the driving force of your life. Let it be your guiding light, a lantern on your life's road. Hope gives you a reason for moving ahead, when it is so easy to fall prey to the present predicament. Hope is the eternal flame. Let hope be your hero to always admire. Take it one step further and embody its essence. LIVE IT!

I took my own advice and did something that I was truly hopeful about, even though I was PETRIFIED! I showed people that my intuitive side was a part of me. If it is a part of you or someone you know, don't be afraid of it! Some people may not approve, but it is not about them, it is about you! Some may surprise you, like I was surprised.

We are on this planet to be happy and make other people happy if it doesn't take away from our own happiness. Look within and you will find your courage to be you. If you have found this, please help someone else you know who is struggling. It all comes back to helping people. HELPING PEOPLE IS MY PASSION!

I always enjoyed helping people in my personal and professional life. My discovery of connecting with spirits, and giving messages to loved ones later in life, continues to be my vocation. If healing can come because of it, this work is *definitely* worth pursuing.

Another aspect of helping is giving. **I FEEL GIVING IS LIVING!** Please think about giving your time, emotion, money, and/or possessions. Whatever the source, give freely and give often. It warms the heart and soothes the soul. I am donating a portion of the proceeds from this book to charities close to my heart. Find your favorites and give. Find a friend or a stranger and give. Giving and helping are intertwined. Make your life and someone else's brighter. Make many lives brighter, and the brilliance shines.

Chapter 34
YouTube Channel

A thought popped into my head about shining a light on professional psychics and people with good intuition. The idea emerged for me to interview them so they could share their experiences, stories, and opinions. I spoke with Sean about it, and he suggested I use YouTube as my platform. He said we could put my shows on podcasts, too. I just "knew" that was the right way to go. Thank you, Sean, for your suggestions!

I feel through the grace of God that I was given the courage to get out of my comfort zone, expose myself to many people, and forge ahead. Once again, I applied my mantra of "Helping people is my passion." I started to think about who I could interview. I contacted people and brainstormed about questions I could ask during an interview. I also felt that the audience should have some input for the show. I came up with the idea of having people submit questions through my website for guests to answer on upcoming shows. I relied on using two questions, in honor of my sister's favorite number.

I needed to come up with a title for the show. The name, *Psychic Connection*, came to me easily, like a lightbulb's illumination. However, I felt I needed something more to hone in on its true purpose. I felt I was guided to a quote that I had used for my "Word of the Day." Every day, I come up with a word and quote with that word that I put on Facebook and Instagram.

The quote I knew I should use was "Collaboration over Competition." I wanted to let the viewers know that psychics didn't have to compete with one another. They can help one another. The title became *Psychic Connection: Collaboration over Competition*. Viewers could tune in and see me interview a variety of guests with a variety of intuitive abilities. Their stories, experiences, and opinions relating to a variety of intuitive topics would be highlighted. Contact information would also be given. Viewers could have one place to go, view the show, and contact a guest if impressed. Sounds like an easy flow, right?

The making of the show was a bit more complicated than I expected, but Sean came to the rescue! He figured out how to create my YouTube channel and put me on various venues for podcasts. He told me that I needed an introductory show before the actual show with guests. He filmed me with his camera for my solo intro. We worked on a type of press release for Facebook, Instagram, and email. I was impressed with his creativity, resourcefulness, and dedication. Do I sound like a proud mother? You bet I do, and rightly so! Remember, I do like to give credit where credit is due. It is one of my expressions of love.

Sean became my producer and editor. I interviewed guests through Zoom. Afterward, Sean and I would review each episode and edit it to approximately thirty minutes. Not an easy task! Sean taught himself to use the editing software, and we both delved into dissecting what should stay and what should go.

Lights, camera, action — tune in Tuesdays! Episodes of *Psychic Connection: Collaboration over Competition* would be ready to view every other Tuesday. The first episode was aired with my tarot card reading brother-in-law, Sal, as my guest. He spoke about his readings, near-death experience, and deceased loved ones. One question I decided to ask each of my guests is about what advice they would give to someone who wants to tap into their intuition or expand it. Sal's suggestion was to take a class, which would be a good way to start. At the end of the show, Sal answered two viewers' questions. I felt the show flowed well with Sal's stories, explanations, and opinions. The reaction to the episode, in my humble opinion, was positive! As I have stated before, with regards to Sean and to other people I talk or write about, I like to give credit where credit is due. Sal was an excellent guest, and the amount of views was proof. Hopefully with more guests coming on, viewers will stay tuned and word will spread for new viewers to get on board.

Chapter 35
It's A Wrap

Please let me pause. If I had gone to a psychic years ago and he or she told me I would do the following:

- Start my own business giving tarot card and medium readings;
- Launch my own website, Facebook page and Instagram;
- Create a YouTube and podcast show, interviewing other professional psychics and people with good intuition;
- Teach classes and host open discussions on intuition;
- Write a book about my psychic medium journey;

I would not have BELIEVED him or her! Of course, I believed in the many psychics I went to see, but for me to actually do all of that? Perhaps I would have reacted like my mother did when the doctor told her she was pregnant. She called him a liar! Remember, though, my mother became blissful when she gave birth to me. My mother loved me with such a strong force.

I also became blissful when I accepted the predictions that became a reality for me and BELIEVED. My intuition and connection with the dead have proven to me that those who pass away continue loving and continue connecting. My mother, even though she has passed, continues to love me fiercely.

LOVE LIVES ON. My *belief is that we don't die.* I believe we shed our bodies and transition to another realm. Our soul, consisting of love and energy, allows us to continue to connect in a different way. To me, the readings prove this. Those who have passed give me messages. I do not come up with them. I am simply the messenger and I know this firsthand. For most clients who I read, I have no prior knowledge of their deceased loved ones. Yet, messages come through that evoke a myriad of emotions for my clients. I have witnessed it, and at times, felt it.

I believe bringing communication, clarity, and most importantly, LOVE to my clients is doing God's work. LIGHT BECOMES LOVE. I feel this strongly in my heart and deep in my soul. I pray more people are open to this possibility, for then they are opening their hearts and souls to love from beyond.

This is gratifying work. I am compelled to share that with you. I love what I do! I agree wholeheartedly with a quote from Aristotle, "The essence of life is to serve others and to do good."

When I use my intuition by reading tarot cards to give guidance to my clients, I feel I help them. When I use my intuition to connect with passed loves ones and share their messages with my clients, I feel I help them. It is difficult to describe this feeling of satisfaction. The allowance of communication between the realms, I believe is a God-given mercy. I have seen the benefits time and time again.

This is my story. My grandmother, all my family, and all the people I have met along the way have contributed to my story. It took me some time to BELIEVE in my intuition and my abilities to connect with spirits, to share their messages. It took me some time to BELIEVE we all live on after we die, somehow, some way. It took me some time to BELIEVE in myself.

I wanted to explain my gifts, stories, and experiences so that others could think about them and draw their own conclusions. Yes, helping people is my passion. I want people to start a thought process about their own mortality and that of others. There are so many theories out there. Who is to say what is right, wrong, or something in the middle? I can only speak for myself.

I pray YOU will question yourself. YOU draw your own conclusions. Yes, YOU in the flesh! While YOU are pondering, please focus on YOU. Please discover YOUR own true passion while YOU are at it. Each one of us has a journey. BELIEVE — DO YOU?

CPSIA information can be obtained
at www.ICGtesting.com
Printed in the USA
JSHW030401300121
11333JS00002B/12